SLAYING
THE GIANT

Uncovering the Things
They Like to Hide

*A doctor's legal battle to save lives
and expose the truth about political
and media corruption during our
nation's opioid epidemic*

D1637239

ISBN 978-1-0980-4075-8 (paperback)
ISBN 978-1-0980-4076-5 (digital)

Christian Faith Publishing, Inc.
832 Park Avenue
Meadville, PA 16335
www.christianfaithpublishing.com

Printed in the United States of America

CONTENTS

ACKNOWLEDGMENT

First, I give glory to God for his many blessings beyond all imagination and comprehension in this lifetime. I give God praise with adoration for my life as I know it now. May I show the love of Christ to everyone I encounter. May I be loving, kind, patient, longsuffering, generous, and encouraging to my family, brothers and sisters in Christ, friends, and strangers who cross my path. May this book, redacted for the privacy of others, provide strength and encouragement to fight fear in our lives. My new motto is "Fear is a liar." Truth only comes from the Word of God. May we seek God's plan for our lives and find strength in His Word.

To my attorney, you really demonstrated your ability to slay the giant! I admired your preparation, expertise, and delivery of the facts of my case to the judge. Your closing arguments really sealed the outcome of the case no matter what the judge decides. I know the truth and you certainly revealed it!

To my dear friends who are fighting similar battles in the name of truth. Watch out for the pit that can appear impossible to surmount. The mucky mire of lies, selfish ambitions, jealousy, corruptness, blame, and cover up may be weighing you down; but in the end, truth wins. Remember, God is bigger than any obstacle thrown your way and with your faith in God, you have the mightiest ally on your side.

To my new colleagues and friends, thank you for welcoming David and me to our new lives out west. I praise God for you every day and I cannot believe we worship, work, live, and play here!

To my wonderful husband, thank you for your support and your love. You stand by me and continue to encourage me daily. I still stand in awe as to where God led us. Big sky country feels like home and we are surrounded by an encouraging church family, friends, and a welcoming community.

To my readers, thank you for your interest in my book. I wrote my first book, *Oh, the Things They Like to Hide*, and this book, *Slaying the Giant, Uncovering the Things They Like to Hide*, to expose hidden opposition in the war involving opioids in our nation. The complex network of political, media, and self-serving leaders in health care make it difficult to do the right thing clinically for our chronic pain patients taking opioids. We simply desire preventing unintentional opioid overdose and death. My story is true. I became a victim, a scapegoat for management and a politician choosing to ignore reports about unintentional deaths occurring at the hospital and in the community related to opioid prescribing practices. Processes put into place to report wrongdoing are tedious and ineffective. It literally takes years to report illegal and unsafe clinical practices by people in positions of power. It takes money (I spent my entire savings), a great attorney, time, energy, patience, persistence, and thick skin to report malpractice, legal offenses, and media misrepresentation. It often takes becoming a whistleblower when leaders retaliate and chaos increases exponentially. I understand many parts of my book are repetitious, but I want to help others and prepare those with similar goals in understanding the never-ending road to truth. You are all reading what David and I endured which included resubmitting, retelling facts, resending evidence, and revisiting the same events over and over again like a bad dream (David's words). My prayers are with any of you who strive to slay giants and uncover the things they like to hide.

PREFACE

Now the God of peace, that brought again from the dead our Lord Jesus, that great shepherd of the sheep, through the blood of the everlasting covenant.

Make you perfect in every good work to do his will, working in you that which is wellpleasing in his sight, through Jesus Christ; to whom be glory for ever and ever, Amen.

—Hebrews 13:20–21 (KJV)

This is a continuation of the true story told in *Oh, the Things They Like to Hide* about politicians, a large health-care system, coercion and how unsolicited political pressure placed upon physicians and providers can thwart efforts to apply opioid safety initiatives in America leading to unintentional drug overdoses. You do not have to read *Oh, the Things They Like to Hide* first, however I do highly recommend reading the book at some point. I will give you enough background to pick you up where those who read the book and I left off.

I battled opioid safety for patients for fifteen years at a large health-care organization to save lives of patients and citizens in the community. When a politician and medical center director entered into the picture with selfish ambitions, they illegally practiced medicine through coercion, threats, and blame. They chose to be blind to the fact that people were overdosing on prescription opioid medications and they chose patient and voter satisfaction over saving lives. The duo ignored truth and embraced self-interest along with selfish ambition. The director and politician threatened clinicians in opposition, using a weak chief of staff as a pawn to potentially take the heat off of their political agendas. Their narcissistic goals collided with patient care. Their greedy pursuits resulted in destruction. The destruction each created ended careers for altruistic health care providers and leaders; created a hostile work environment for remaining employees; resulted in a shortage of physicians to care for patients; and worse yet, led to loss of life for patients at the facility and in the community. This is my story.

Background and Introduction

The LORD knoweth the days of the upright: and
their inheritance shall be forever.
—Psalm 37:18 (KJV)

First, let's begin with my background. I attended medical school at
the age of thirty, a time when everyone thought this was too old to
pursue such a lofty career. I defied the allopathic (MD) schools after
multiple rejections due to my age and other political influences at
that time which pales to my current story so we will skip that part
of my life. The Osteopathic Medicine School in the land of wheat
field farmers welcomed me with open arms during my site interview
visit. Two weeks later, I was on my way to medical school in my little
Chevy Sprint. I packed my car fully, every square inch of the interior
filled with my possessions. Four years later, I graduated third in my
class which began with 171 students.

Following further training, I served in the military as a general
medical officer. I raised my hand taking the oath to serve my country
during the first Gulf War and my mom cried. I always yearned to
serve my country in the armed forces since childhood. I felt for those
who fought in the war. Vietnam was such a terrible place to serve. So
much tragedy. Brave men and women served only to come home to
a country who spat on them. I wanted to take care of them, initially
as a counselor or psychiatrist. I was driven to fulfill this dream.

Stationed at a submarine base on the coast, I enjoyed working
as a general medical officer in the Acute Care Clinic treating active
duty service members, their families, and retirees. When I completed

my service obligation, I sought after my dream of solo general medical practice in a small tourist town on the east coast. After one year of being "on call," twenty-four seven on-call, 365 days per year, I wanted out. I stayed three more years. I loved my patients and I did not want to leave them. Eventually, I had to leave them because there was nothing left of me. I gave my everything to everyone else and I knew I had to find some support elsewhere.

I went home for Christmas in December of 2001. Home at the time and for most of my life was on the great lakes. My mom still lives there. Most of my friends reside in that area as did my husband, David. I had not met David yet. He comes into my life a little later, but not much later. I thought to myself at that time, "well, I loved being a military doctor, so why don't I check out the large health-care system?" I walked into the hospital and asked about opportunities. I was basically hired on the spot. I ran into the right people at the right time in the Human Resources Department. The next day I interviewed with the chief of staff and others. Finally, I would be part of a group of physicians with a support system and no "on call" as an outpatient physician for two outpatient clinics (OCs). I felt relieved and rejuvenated.

I found a wonderful Baptist church during my first visit home, so I knew I would have a church family. After a long day, I sat at my mom's house discussing the day and future plans. The phone rang. It was David, the man my mom wanted to fix me up with, but I was resisting at the moment. He sounded nice. He invited me out for coffee. I hesitated because I was leaving for the east coast early the next morning. I agreed to meet him for coffee. The coffee shop was closed so we went to the bar next door and drank coffee…for hours.

I drove back to the east coast. It was hard to go back; but it had to be done. David called me that night and almost every night since. We have been happily married for eighteen years now.

Following a year of fighting for justice and subsequent turmoil the battle created, I am now working in the private sector as a primary care physician. I don't want to get too ahead of myself so please allow me further reflection.

I served as a large health-care system employee for over fifteen years at three locations, Great Lakes Medical Center, a facility in the land of cornfields and soybeans, and Facility by the River Health Care System. Following eight years as a primary care provider, I sought leadership training desiring to advocate for front line clinical staff, employees who directly serve patients. I thought if we treat our staff right, they will be able to care for the patients. This thought, although achievable in premise, proved to lead to my demise at the large health-care system. Wouldn't you think honest people could be servant leaders in health-care? Ha! I laugh at my ignorance and lofty impossible goals now.

My last location and job for the large health-care system landed me at Facility by the River Health Care System (FBTHRHCS). Appointed associate chief of staff and opioid safety initiative facility champion, I oversaw primary care at six different physical locations. Other clinical employees such as physicians, pharmacists, social workers, nurses, and others sought my expert opinion regarding the application of opioid safety initiatives regularly. With years of experience and participation in national and regional opioid safety committees, others consulted with me. We applied opioid safety initiatives at our facility and we made tremendous progress. We saved lives.

Unfortunately, many of the patients receiving opioids for chronic pain complained about safety changes. Instead of being grateful that we were saving their lives, they complained, even when they were not doing safe things with their opioids. Some of the patients were found to be chewing their fentanyl patches, crushing and snorting their pills, selling their pills to others in the community, stockpiling their pills, doctor shopping at over a dozen other medical offices and emergency departments (EDs), using up their supplies too quickly, combining opioids with other unsafe medications including illegal substances, or taking high quantities of opioids with serious medical conditions predisposing them to unintentional overdose and death. Some of the patients died.

I reported unsafe use of opioid medication to our new director in the fall of 2016. He failed to listen to me. I persisted and presented the director with supporting documents including newspaper reports of arrested patients, hospital documents regarding patients hospitalized in the community due to unintentional overdoses, our findings of deaths related to unintentional overdoses at our hospital, and reports from the state Prescription Monitoring Program (seventy-two of them) illustrating unsafe practices by our patients. The chief of staff scolded me like a child for attempting to disclose my concerns which were unsafe and often illegal. What was going on?!

I learned the director despised any attention he received politically and publicly. When a television news story hit our area regarding opioid safety negatively, the director's anger rose. In short, the news story displayed me as the doctor "cutting off all the patients at the knees" and the chief of staff basically "threw me under the bus" in the news story. All the while, my smiling face flashed across the television screen, demonizing my opioid safety intentions.

The next day, headquarters became involved. The news story essentially blamed me personally and the article rose to the top three national stories involving the organization. Wow! What an accomplishment. Electronic messages started flying. Telephones rang. What was this all about? Who was this Dr. Sky? Why was this allowed to happen? Didn't the director have control of his facility? What role did the chief of staff play? I don't think I know half of all that happened. You see, I was on leave for two weeks recertifying for my family medicine boards and interviewing for another position at different large health-care hospital on the coast.

On my way home from the east coast, I learned about the television news story. I grew ill. David and I just bought a house by the shore and we looked forward to a new chapter in our lives following a job promotion offered by another facility. The news story changed our lives. Looking back, we praise God for his divine intervention; but at the time, the situation devastated us.

I returned to Facility by the River Health Care System and endured an interview by the Accountability Office to the Ignorant Oversight Body. To my genuine surprise and later dismay, I became the subject of the investigation! What? Me? The interviewers asked me about being disciplined for my actions regarding opioid safety initiatives. I laughed initially. Silence. Oh no, they were serious. I said, "Seriously?" I stated other leaders said I deserved a medal for my efforts and I just received a high midterm rating two weeks ago. What changed?

I learned during that interview that the chief of staff committed perjury and completely lied about my opioid safety leadership efforts. I failed to comprehend why he would lie. Was I missing something? Surely this could be corrected. I was wrong.

Two days later, I received a summary suspension of my privileges citing, "concerns have been raised to suggest that aspects of (my) clinical practice do not meet the accepted standards of practice and potentially constitute an imminent threat to patient welfare." Additionally, the allegation stated, "Failure to implement opioid safety initiative with patients in a safe and ethical manner." After a flood of disbelief, confusion, denial, and later anger, the battle was on.

I researched my options to fight this unbelievable war which ensued from altruistic intentions of helping our country save lives from unintentional overdoses. For fifteen years, I served as a provider and leader of this all-important effort. I consulted and wrote letters to many oversight bodies and committees. I contacted the Hassle-Free Office, Equal Rights Organization, Complaint Department Office, Grievance Division Office, Subcommittee on Oversight and Investigation, and Legal Battle Board. Intimately involved with my case, I pressed on writing letters, answering inquiries, supplying documentation supporting my claims, and working to prove my innocence.

Early in the fight, I secured an attorney who helped me with reinstatement of my privileges, but the process took too long and I lost my position at the East Coast Medical Center. When I realized this fight was becoming more of a battle, I had to find another attorney. After much research and multiple telephone calls, I found the right firm. They "got it!" They completely understood the battleground, obstacles, and the enemy. My attorneys understood the underlying political influences which complicated the battle for truth. Moreover, the law firm attorneys believed the facility used me as an innocent scapegoat in retaliation to an unseen war involving political power and position. Victory number one, they believed me and understood me. Hallelujah!

Employees of the organization received annual training about their rights should the company impose discriminatory, illegal, or retaliatory acts upon an employee. I suffered from all of the above and I knew the organization violated their own expectations. The war began.

I first filed a complaint with the Equal Rights Organization. I filled out lengthy forms citing multiple violations related to my gender and age. The first step involved contact with an ERO counselor and took place in the spring of 2017. A formal complaint was then filed on the proper form and submitted. I alleged practices and policies that were violated and affected terms, conditions, and privileges of employment. I included the humiliating news story. I disclosed the unlawful release of my photograph by the director. Lastly, I outlined the retaliatory act by the director of suspending my clinical privileges against the advice of the Professional Standards Board and Clinical Executive Board resulting in the loss of my position at the East Coast Medical Center, an advancement opportunity for my career.

I filed a complaint that discrimination took place when I was subjected to a hostile work environment based upon sex and age in the new year of 2017. I endured forty-five minutes of ridicule, harassment and personal humiliation from angry patients during a professional development conference while the director stood by and smiled. At least seventy-five of my colleagues witnessed the harassment. Additionally, I endured humiliation at weekly morning reports and leadership meetings by the director in front of twenty or so leaders. The suspension of my clinical privileges resulted due to retaliatory actions imposed by the director two days after the television news story aired. As a result of the suspension of my privileges, I could no longer provide patient care, serve as associate chief of staff for primary care, or serve as the opioid safety champion for the facility or large health care system.

The Equal Rights Organization accepted the case for investigation stating my position of employment met the standard of being "sufficiently related to the overall pattern of harassment and will be included for consideration in the analysis of the harassment claim." The ERO determined my claim of harassment to pass "the severe or pervasive requirement for further processing." The response by the ERO stated, "The actions taken against your client by senior management establishes a pattern of conduct that could create a hostile work environment and /or that could interfere with the job performance of a reasonable person." Multiple claims were independently accepted. I felt relieved. Someone listened.

Ultimately, I could not afford attorney fees for pursing this avenue of justification. I had to choose which path to pursue and the Legal Battle Board proved to be the way to go. Grateful to be validated in the ERO pursuit, I made my choice to end this road to victory with a peace that passed all understanding.

I also filed a complaint to the Grievance Division Office in the spring of 2017. This group deals with complaints of reprisal and retaliation for whistleblowing activities as a prohibited personnel practice. The director certainly retaliated against my disclosures of patient wrong doing. The director retaliated against me for reporting illegal acts performed by both the director and chief of staff. They coerced the primary care providers to reinstate opioids to known addicts, patients who were selling or misusing their opioids, and patients who had medical problems putting them at risk for respiratory depression and death. I later learned the director also retaliated against me due to his embarrassment following the news story stating, "staple the damn news story to her suspension."

The Grievance Division Office accepted my case. An attorney was assigned to investigate. After our initial conversation and exchange of information, a long silence in communication resulted. I later learned she suffered a personal tragedy when her communication resumed many months later. By this time, my attorney took over and interacted with this group on my behalf.

I filed a complaint with the Complaint Department Office based upon disclosure of wrongdoing pertaining to violation of a law, rule, or regulation; gross mismanagement; a gross waste of funds; an abuse of authority; and a substantial and specific danger to public health or safety. My complaint fit most of these requirements for acceptance into an investigation. I wrote the following letter to the Complaint Department Office:

I am a board-certified family practice physician, former Naval general medical officer with four years in private solo practice and fifteen years at the organization. I have fifteen years of experience addressing opioid safety initiatives at the organization, first as a primary care provider for eight years, primary specialty service line director developing a multidisciplinary pain management group for a facility for five years, and associate chief of staff for primary care charged with initiating opiate safety initiatives (OSI) as the facility OSI champion along with a pain psychologist for two years. I was recruited by this facility because of my leadership, pain management clinic development, and opiate safety initiative experiences.

OSI efforts all fall onto primary care at this facility. I am an advocate for primary care providers across the facility as the associate chief of staff for primary care, opioid safety initiative (OSI) champion prescriber for the facility, and OSI representative for the region for pain management. Our efforts in primary care in applying opioid safety initiatives efforts were highly supported by the chief of staff and service line leaders including but not limited to pharmacy, mental health, acute medicine, prosthetics, extended care and rehabilitation chiefs. The newly appointed chief of staff, previously deputy chief of staff, had minimal to no knowledge of pain management and opioid safety initiatives until I arrived. As previously stated, this is one of the reasons I was recruited to this facility.

One city in the river state and one of our rural clinics were outliers in number of opioids dispensed. The Drug Enforcement Agency (DEA) investigated our facility at the end of 2015. Another investigation body investigated our facility in the spring 2016. This same city also has one of the greatest populations of unintentional overdoses in the country. Prior to my arrival in the fall of 2015, there was minimal application of OSI requirements except for completion of pain agreements. Primary care providers did not have much leadership support since the primary care leaders were assigned to care for patients due to a large exodus of primary care providers from the facility. Since my arrival, the facility has been educated on interpretation of urine drug screens, pharmacy database access and use, use of pill counts, use of clinical pharmacy specialists to assist in tapering, OSI education, and more. All the patients on opioids received a letter to explain opioid safety initiatives to prevent unintentional overdoses in the spring of 2016. Political partners received a letter to explain OSI intentions in the spring of 2016. Our providers, nursing staff, and administrative staff for primary care spent hours on the telephone speaking with patients about opiate safety. Face-to-face discussions are encouraged at every visit. Unfortunately, some patients remain unsatisfied. We are working to continue to improve our services both at this facility and through networking in the community. We now provide prosthetic devices to help with pain, chiropractic care, acupuncture, aqua therapy, physical therapy, physiatry, and other nonnarcotic medications for pain and more. All of our efforts have been reported back to the investigating officials.

As opioid safety co-champion along with the pain psychologist and associate chief of staff for primary care, I assist with chart reviews as requested by the chief of staff, primary care providers, pharmacists, other medical providers, nurses, administrative staff, and others often offering recommendations to consider or help with interpretation of test results, etc. If a provider is on leave, I will often assist with renewals of opioids since we do not have a pain management department prescriber, although this is in the works. With my fifteen years of experience in this field, I can offer suggestions in many if not most cases. I partner with the clinical pharmacy specialist for tapers. Some patients do not need tapers if there is no opioid in the urine on the drug screen and the opioid is simply not renewed. Mental health providers are co-located in primary care and we have a warm handoff policy to assist any patient in need. Our efforts have greatly increased over the past eighteen months since my arrival.

I earned the respect of many of my colleagues serving in positions of leadership. I earned the respect of pharmacists, primary care providers, specialty providers, nurses, and clerical staff. My goal has been to advocate for clinical staff with the thought that if they feel supported, they will take good care of the patients. Primary care scored very high on our employee survey (ES) and the results were exciting.

The director started at the organization at the end of fiscal year 2016. Our primary care service leaders presented OSI history, goals, and accomplishments on numerous occasions to the director and executive leadership staff. Our primary care service explained the primary care turnover concerns in the past, our challenges, and our recent successes. We are almost fully staffed in all locations once our recent hires start soon. Access for care is our goal; same-day access and we are almost there. To retain primary care providers, I stopped overbooking upon my arrival and negotiated for administrative time weekly. Overbooking and lack of administrative time leads to provider and clinical staff burnout and turnover. Recently, the director made the decision to restart overbooks for primary care providers and this was implemented while I was away on leave in the spring of 2017. Additionally, the chief of staff participated on a television news interview where my name was used repeatedly, my photograph was shown without my permission violating policy, and my professional and personal reputation was disparaged. I learned about the news story airing while driving home back from leave at the end of the spring in 2017. I participated in OSI educational programs on the radio in the past and I was the person contacted by the news station initially. I later learned that this was not to be a friendly interview. I declined; but the chief of staff participated. The chief of staff had been supportive of our opioid safety initiative efforts for the entire eighteen months I had been at this facility. I had a midterm evaluation early spring of 2017 and was rated as fully successful. I was rated as outstanding on my fiscal year 2016 proficiency citing opiate safety initiative accomplishments as a major factor. Our efforts in primary care, although difficult to measure, have helped in the prevention of unintentional overdoses for patients and the community. We still have much work to do in our efforts.

On a Wednesday in the spring, the city paper published a very unflattering article. The politician is quoted vilifying our facility and the organization in general based upon one-sided deceptive reports by untruthful patients. Many politicians contact our facility on behalf of patients. This is standard practice. Primary care leadership reaches out to the patients on behalf of the facility regarding opioid safety concerns. We are a knowledgeable team. We provide the written responses to the official inquiries. One politician however, has been relentless. She continuously "over advocates" for patients not understanding their clinical history and she ultimately coerces the executive leadership team of the facility, most notably the director (no clinical knowledge) and chief of staff, to act upon inaccurate clinical reports. The chief of staff in turn oftentimes asks me for chart reviews and recommendations; but with continued pressure by the politician and the director, both without clinical knowledge, the chief of staff has been reported to approach primary care providers without my knowledge to "reconsider the opioid plan." Often, I am notified by these providers and/or pharmacists who fill the prescriptions that they are feeling coerced into doing something unsafe and illegal for the patients, which could result in unintentional overdose and death. Specific examples can be shared.

The television news story aired and featured three patients stating that patients were "cut off" with no communication and the politician ridiculed opioid safety efforts by the organization. The story also featured the chief of staff for a facility who made ill-informed comments about facility provider practices, which I found surprising since he supported of our OSI efforts all along. Additionally, the chief of staff had been positively recognized, along with the director, for our OSI best practices at the facility. I have the documentation to prove why opioids were stopped for safety on the three interviewed patients. The politician, newscaster, and chief of staff failed to check facts prior to airing the story. These facts, of course, may not be shared publicly due to HIPAA rules, which was one of the reasons I declined the interview.

My name was used extensively in a derogatory manner during the airing of the story on the news. As previously mentioned, the director released my photograph without my permission, violating policy and the television news story flashed my photograph throughout the story. As opioid safety provider champion for the facility and associate chief of staff for primary care with fifteen years of primary care, pain management, and opioid safety experience at the organization, I would be the physician that staff consulted for advice. Chart review is a standard practice for champions and associate chief of staff to use and involved reviewing the state prescription monitoring program site, medication list, opioid agreement, urine drug screen, pill counts, radiographs, provider note history, and other appropriate information. When the urine does not have the drug in the urine and the patient is filling that opioid in the community and at the facility regularly, the opioid agreement (reviewed and signed by the patient previously) has been violated. It is standard practice not to renew opioids at the facility or in the community if the opioid agreement is violated. Patients are informed of the findings by a primary team member in a respectful manner. Additional care is offered.

At the end of the spring, I returned to work from leave. The following day, I received a summary suspension of privileges citing aspects of my practice "do not meet the excepted standard of practice and constitute an imminent threat to patient welfare." I understand the director ordered the chief of staff to recommended immediate summary suspension of privileges in response to public embarrass-ment and political pressure, abusing his authority as director. The chief of staff agreed and issued a summary suspension of privileges, abusing his authority as chief of staff. Issuing a summary of privi-leges is warranted only when "sufficient evidence exists, based on the preliminary fact-finding, that a practitioner may have demonstrated substandard care, professional misconduct or patient care." The director and chief of staff failed to follow procedures and processes clearly outlined in the medical staff bylaws and rules of the organiza-tion and policies pertaining to credentialing and privileging. Actions by the director and chief of staff were carried out in haste and retal-iation in response to public embarrassment and political pressure.

Primary care providers at the facility presently do not have a supportive leader or opioid safety initiative champion provider to consult regarding opioid safety concerns. Several of the strong eth-ical providers, unwilling to be coerced by the director and the chief of staff, are now being targeted for removal from employment. An ethical provider at a contract site was recently given an employment opportunity at the facility. I understood that the employment offer was going to be rescinded and indeed it was rescinded, again reflecting the political environment and abuse of authority by leaders previously mentioned. The physician is a highly respected leader in the community.

Many of the service line leaders and chiefs reported concerns that their privileges and employment may be terminated at the whim and abuse of authority by the director and chief of staff succumbing to public embarrassment and political pressure.

Lastly, there is a substantial danger to public health and safety if the organization and the community fail to initiate and uphold opioid safety measures. Leaders, political representatives, and others have the right to inquire about their patients' and citizens' concerns. These concerns are routinely investigated and communicated to the patient and office submitting the inquiry as part of our daily work in the primary care administrative office. The leaders, political representatives, and others do not have the right to abuse their positions of authority and coerce physicians to prescribe or treat patients when the providers know their recommendations may result in iatrogenic harm to patients including unintentional overdose and death related to opioid prescribing. Nonclinical leaders, political representatives, and others do not know the clinical background of the patients and citizens they serve. Clinicians know the clinical history of the patients and citizens they serve. Leaders, political representatives, and others do not have the right to abuse their positions of authority to suspend a provider's privileges, rescind employment offers, or threaten termination of an employee based upon misleading reports.

The city in the river state that had the highest rate of unintentional overdoses in the state is also one of the highest across the country. We owe it to our patients and community citizens to prevent unintentional overdoses and risk of death related to opioids. The Centers for Disease Control guideline for prescribing opioids for chronic pain is our major source for OSI guidance and goals as a nation. The leader of the organization put out guidance regarding opioid safety initiative updates. The organization has an opioid safety toolkit to use for guidance with a multitude of resources. These professional clinical references and others have been used extensively over the past eighteen months at the facility under the primary care and OSI champion leadership in collaboration with other service line leaders, clinical pharmacy specialists, pain psychology champions, and others with full support by the chief of staff until recently.

To mention, I am a wartime Veteran who served as a general medical officer (GMO) for the US Navy stateside. My son is an Iraqi wartime combat Veteran suffering from wartime disabilities. He would have been homeless without my husband's and my support. He receives care presently at the organization.

Respectfully submitted,

Dr. B. Sky

Both the Complaint Department Office and Grievance Division Office accepted my case and assigned attorneys for investigation. With relief, my attorney communicated on my behalf and navigated the two agencies. In the end, the two groups turned my case over to the Legal Battle Board which supposedly had more power.

It is laughable at best that I write about the Legal Battle Board. The Appeals Board of the Legal Battle Board (which becomes important later) should be composed of three appointed members to make legal decisions about cases. Two of the three positions are presently unoccupied and the third member will be retiring this year. He presently works on cases full time; but the cases sit in a room, unresolved because two board positions are unoccupied. I understand there is no sense of urgency to appoint members and this is all politically influenced. Imagine that...

CHAPTER 1

Peace at Last

The LORD bless thee, and keep thee: The LORD
make his face shine upon thee, and be gracious
unto thee: The LORD lift up his countenance
upon thee, and give thee peace.
                                    —Numbers 6:24–26 (KJV)

I wonder why I waited so long to return to private practice. The difference in navigating the private medical world astonishes me. There are now many outpatient positions without "on call." Despite all of the publicity that follows me, I had employment opportunities in the end. Initially, I felt beaten up, hopeless, and shameful until I realized I did not create this state of affairs. I participated in opioid safety as part of the solution. I applied my experience and shared lessons learned, best practices, and supported primary care providers and others of the medical staff.

The Lord truly blessed us with a relocation to the big sky country out west. We live in a house on a hill, my dream ever since I can remember. Our home looks like a lodge with mountain views from every window. Tall pine trees loom alongside the aspens. A creek filled with trout bubbles through our property below creating soothing sounds of comfort as we appreciate God's work of nature.

My husband continues to drive me to work every day and others have fun calling me "princess." I fondly remember another "princess" from my time spent at the Facility by the River Health Care System and her encouragement. I smile. I praise God for all of the storms and for bringing David and me to where we now live. We rejoice and remind each other that all of the previous turmoil and suffering will result in God's glory. I love caring for patients on a full-time basis once again. My four-day work week allows David and me to explore the western frontier. There are real cowboys out here!

David and I settled into big sky country as if we were born and raised here. The small-town life, filled with social friendly folk, welcomed us like family. Many of my patients attend my church and I care for many of my church family as their family doctor. It works out here. It is easy to establish boundaries creating a work life balance. The community holds many events such as rodeos, barbeques, painting parties, lobster fests (believe it or not), Christmas strolls through town, and other creative events. It is fun to attend gatherings because we know so many people in attendance. The small friendly local newspaper captures the events and we are often in the social section. I am no longer a news story victim. I am now a cherished neighbor and friend. These are just a few of the blessings God bestowed upon us.

We live in a small community with Mennonites. The community comes together in the autumn for a fall festival. We all bring a dish to share and a large pot of simmering goodness sits in the middle of the gathering. The food melts in your mouth. We all hang out and talk like family. It's a bit chilly and fires are lit to warm us and the light shines brightly on our faces. The Dinnerbell is in the background, owned by dear Mennonite friends. The famous restaurant attracts people from all over the state for the weekly all-you-can-eat chicken dinner with scrumptious fixings and homemade pie with ice cream for dessert.

This winter was a doozy. We had subzero temperatures for days and snow piled high over six feet deep. David drove us into the ditch trying to pull over for passing church goers just as I screamed, "slow down we're heading for the d i t c h......" Bam! We slid and ended up sideways with David suspended in the air and I landed on the bottom. Our neighbors came to the rescue. Many altruistic people stopped to help. It is just the way it is out here. I shouted praise to the Lord and hugged everyone involved in getting us out of that mess.

David heard about it for weeks. I told everyone about the ditch episode; but I heard unexpected replies. Instead of laughing at us, most people replied, "when you live in big sky country, everyone ends up in a ditch sometime." This relieved David and quickly shut me up.

Guns are big out here and a necessity. We have mountain lions, black bears, grizzlies, moose, and other wild animals roaming our property. Cats and dogs are bait. Most people carry a gun outdoors for protection. Guns have been needed indoors also. A new friend of mine had a bear break into his home and he was able to scare it away. Another co-worker had a mountain lion on his porch guarding the prey he just killed and hid in his flower garden. The prey was the neighbor's dog. Sad.

One of the big events in town is the NRA dinner and auction. Everyone in town attends and friends invited us at the last minute. The hosts displayed guns for auction throughout the event center. Little guns, big guns, pink guns, blue guns, shotguns, rifles, revolvers, 9mm handguns…so many to see. We still don't own a gun, but I believe we need one. We carry bear spray like a gun; but this may not work on some wild animals. Recently, a man survived a cougar attack by strangling it. Two other men were camping and a mountain lion attacked one. While the other man ran away, the lion chased him and dragged him to the den. A ranger was riding his bicycle down the mountain, came upon a grizzly with her cub and she swiped him, killing him instantly. One of my patients suffered from two different grizzly attacks while hunting. One grizzly wanted his prized elk situated on the four-wheeler and knocked the four-wheeler over, swiping at him continuously as he scrambled to avoid fatal injuries. Eventually, the grizzly left and my patient called a friend for help. On another occasion, my patient surprised a grizzly bear who had hidden a meal nearby. The grizzly clamped down on his right arm as he defended himself, breaking his arm. His gun was at his right side, but the fracture left his arm unusable. I don't remember how he survived; but thankfully, he did. My neighbors know all about my patient's two encounters because nothing is kept secret in small communities. A close neighbor actually was the person my patient called to help him. Amazing. These are true stories. Some people survive attacks.

Others don't. I realize guns create controversy; but out here, they are part of everyday life and survival. So, with this in mind, events such as the NRA dinner are cherished and enjoyed.

Many of our neighbors included us in their celebrations with friends and family. We attended a Christmas celebration, Saint Patrick's Day party, Cinco de Mayo birthday party, New Year's Eve party, and other gatherings. David and I realized we hadn't socialized this much throughout our entire married life. Somehow, the pressure of my job at the large health-care system zapped our energy. We settled in survival mode for years. Worse yet, we failed to notice. Big sky country and God's blessing set us back on fire.

Last summer, visitor season arrived following winter. My mom, dad, brother, aunt, uncle, and cousin visited with their families. David's mother, David's brother and family, our sons, friends from the cornfields and soybeans, and coworkers from the river state stopped by for a visit. We all explored Glacier Park, Yellowstone, and the quaint town of Ennis (where our favorite artist lives, David Lemon). My mother-in-law rejoiced at the opportunity to meet David Lemon in person and so did we. We are now friends on Facebook I might add. Such a thrill! Some of our visitors enjoyed day trips through the mountains on four wheelers. What a blast! And so scenic too... all right outside our driveway. We have seen black bears, moose, elk, white tail deer, mule deer, eagles, and other wildlife on our outings (which is why we really should carry a gun). My cousin's husband expressed that the mountain ride was one of the best things he had ever done. Instant joy flooded my heart.

Winter visitors enjoy our lodge-like home also. My brother, his family, and their neighbors visited midwinter. The kids enjoyed sledding down our hill. I enjoyed taking photographs of them with huge smiles on their faces as they passed by me on their sleds. They all enjoyed a local ski resort during the day and came back early because the kids wanted to play in the snow more than they wanted to ski. How fun. They built a huge igloo from a mound of snow and lit up the tunnels with lights. As I watched the joyful group of children, I reminisced about my childhood in Minnesota. I still love snow and the crunch under my feet in subzero temperatures. I think it is funny when my nose hairs freeze outdoors too. Silly.

My job brings me peace and joy. With all of the chaos at the large health-care system, I forgot that peace and joy were possible. Sure, I relied on the Lord and He proved faithful and I survived an ordeal I never dreamed possible. I guess I forgot to ask Him for peace and joy. He gave it to me anyway in His own time. His perfect time. I doubt I would have recognized the many blessings and maybe I missed the blessings in the past because I chose to wallow in grief or merely survive from day to day. Either way, I see the blessings now. The administrators treat the clinicians with respect. They exude integrity that the leaders of the large health-care system bragged about but did not possess. I am able to advocate for patients and my efforts are well received, even appreciated. I can get radiographs, lab work, consultations, and treatment plans in place in a day instead of two weeks, two months, or two years. A jaundiced patient with severe nausea, vomiting, and abdominal pain, who was camping in the area on vacation, presented to the clinic. The lab work, MRCP radiographic study, consultation to the gastroenterologist, and ERCP procedure by the specialist were completed within one day. The patient recovered quickly, and he was able to continue his vacation with minimal complications if any. I marveled at what our small rural hospital could accomplish. There was no red tape to fight, no obstacles to cross, no waiting to endure, and no frustration to feel.

Doctor's day just passed. Our administrative board gave us Yeti cups with our names on them. I appreciated this gesture of remembrance, appreciation, and thoughtfulness. I enjoy participating in hospital events because I feel valued. I participate in community events, fundraisers, chamber meetings, and other events on behalf of the hospital because I feel appreciated and I enjoy attending. No longer am I forced to attend hostile meetings. I attend because I desire to attend. Refreshing!

CHAPTER 2

Telling My Side of the Story, the Truth as I Honestly Told with Christ as My Witness

Only fear the LORD, and serve him in truth with all your heart; for consider how great (things)he hath done for you.

—1 Samuel 12:24 (KJV)

The next step in my battle was to prepare for the legal proceedings. This preparation took many hours. I helped my attorney prepare for my case which proved to be therapeutic in the end. This is the polished formal statement submitted by my brilliant attorney, redacted of course:

LEGAL BATTLE BOARD
HEADQUARTERS

BAILEY B. SKY,	2017-XXXXX
Appellant,	DOCKET NO.:
	xxx-xx-xxx-xxxx
v.	
LARGE HEALTH-CARE SYSTEM	
Agency	

Hon. Mr. Judge
Administrative Judge

Date: New Year 2018

APPELLANT'S RESPONSE TO ORDER ON JURISDICTION
AND PROOF REQUIREMENTS

Appellant, by and through her undersigned counsel, hereby
submits this response to the Order on Jurisdiction and Proof
Requirements dated Early New Year 2018.

I.   FACTUAL BACKGROUND

Dr. B. Sky was until recently the Associate Chief of Staff of
Primary Care at the Facility by the River Health Care System
("FBTRHCS") and in charge of overseeing FBTRHCS's primary
care providers. Dr. Sky, a veteran and mother of a veteran, began
her position at FBTRHCS in the fall off 2015 after 17 years of prior
service. During her service at FBTRHCS Dr. Sky also held the role
of Opioid Safety Initiative Facility Co-Champion for FBTRHCS.

Dr. Sky's first line supervisor was FBTRHCS Chief of Staff, Dr.
CoS, and her second line supervisor was FBTRHCS Mr. Director.
Because the prescription of opioids at FBTRHCS is largely handled
by primary care physicians, Dr. Sky was the main point of interface
between the frontline physicians prescribing opioids and FBTRHCS's
top management.

Despite the growing realization that over-prescription of opioids has become a nationwide epidemic, efforts to solve the problem
can still generate vocal opponents. Specifically, patients whose opioid
prescriptions are being tapered (i.e., gradually reduced) or suspended
(i.e., cut off completely) are frequently unhappy; in many cases
because they are addicted. More perniciously, a few patients actively
divert opioids (i.e., sell medication rather than take it themselves)
and react extremely negatively when their supply is cut off.

Between Dr. Sky's arrival and the spring of 2017, FBTRHCS physicians began prescribing fewer opioids; which created a backlash among patients whose prescriptions were being tapered or suspended. The Medical Center's top officials, Mr. Director and Dr. Chief of Staff, are highly sensitive to public criticism of the facility and their job evaluations are directly tied to evaluation of patient satisfaction—creating a strong incentive for them to give "loud" patients what they want regardless of the costs to patients' health and community safety.

Since her arrival at FBTRHCS, Dr. Sky has repeatedly disclosed instances where FBTRHCS's actions were contributing to the opioid crisis as described specifically in Section II below. Those disclosures stood in the way of Mr. Director and Dr. Chief of Staff's efforts to prioritize "patient satisfaction" over the health and safety of patients, leading directly to the retaliatory acts described in Section III.

As described more fully below, reducing opioid over-prescription was and is both necessary for patient and community safety, but unpopular with the patients taking those opioids. Dr. Sky's numerous opioid related disclosures made her a target for FBTRHCS leadership, particularly when they were placed under pressure by unhappy patients, and she was targeted for retaliation as a result.

II.   LEGAL STANDARD

"The Board has jurisdiction over an appeal based on whistleblower reprisal under policy if the appellant has exhausted his administrative remedies before the Grievance Division Office and makes non-frivolous allegations of the following: (1) she engaged in whistleblowing activity by making a protected disclosure; and (2) the disclosure was a contributing factor in the agency's decision to take or fail to take a personnel action.

III.   EXHAUSTION OF GDO REMEDIES

Dr. Sky submitted a complaint to the Grievance Division Office (GDO) in the spring of 2017 and amended that complaint in the fall of 2017. Exhibit A; Exhibit B. The GDO terminated its investigation of Dr. Sky's complaints later in the fall of 2017. Exhibit C. As outlined in the attached Exhibit D (GDO Correspondence) and Exhibit E (GDO Appeals) Dr. Sky raised all of the issues discussed herein with the GDO. Therefore, Dr. Sky has properly exhausted her administrative remedies as to all claims, disclosures, acts of retaliation, and arguments addressed herein.

IV. LIST OF PROTECTED DISCLOSURES, DATES, INDIVIDUALS, AND REASONABLE BELIEF IN THE TRUTH OF THOSE DISCLOSURES

Protected whistleblowing occurs when an appellant makes a disclosure that he reasonably believes evidences a violation of law, rule, or regulation, gross mismanagement, a gross waste of funds, an abuse of authority, or a substantial and specific danger to public health or safety. At the jurisdictional stage, the appellant is only burdened with non-frivolously alleging that he reasonably believed that his disclosure evidenced a violation of one of the circumstances described in U.S.C. §.

Under legal acts, disclosures "made to a supervisor or to a person who participated in an activity that the employee or applicant reasonably believed to be covered, reveal[ing] information that had been previously disclosed," made verbally, or made during the normal course of duties of the employee may all qualify as protected disclosures. In other words, Dr. Sky's repeated statements telling her first and second-line supervisors that specific actions those supervisors were undertaking were improper count as protected disclosures.

A.   Disclosure A: Reporting Patient Misuse of Opioids Prescribed by FBTRHCS

Dr. Sky disclosed on multiple occasions to Dr. Chief of Staff and Mr. Director that FBTRHCS patients were taking prescription opioids inappropriately or were diverting opioids that had been prescribed to them. In many cases she disclosed that those patients were allowed to continue taking opioids in violation of state law, sound medical practice, and patient safety.

In the cases of patients diverting their prescriptions, she disclosed that these patients were almost certainly selling those prescription opioids and contributing to the ongoing local opioid epidemic.

1.   When Was the Disclosure Made?

Winter 2015, Spring 2016, Summer 2016, Fall 2016, Winter 2017 (Note that the dates are not exhaustive and Dr. Sky disclosed similar instances many times since 2015.)

2.   To Whom (Name and Title) Was the Disclosure Made?

Mr. Medical Center Director and Dr. Medical Center Chief of Staff

3.   Disclosure of Information Evidenced:

a.   Violation of Law, Rule, or Regulation

It is a felony offense to dispense a controlled substance outside the scope of professional practice and not for a legitimate medical purpose. U.S.C. The term "dispense" is defined to include to doctors prescribing controlled substances. U.S.C. §. To be valid, a prescription for a controlled substance must be issued for a legitimate medical purpose by a practitioner acting in the usual course of medical practice. C.F.R. The State Court of Appeals recently affirmed that a physician can be charged with reckless homicide for prescribing prescription drugs "without medical purpose and outside the usual course of practice."

Physicians are disciplined by state medical boards, have DEA registrations revoked, and are charged with crimes every day for participating in "pill mill" prescribing practices. Tell-tale evidence of wrongdoing includes prescribing when a patient's urine drug screen is negative, and prescribing even when the patient obtains multiple prescriptions from multiple providers. Additionally, a recipe for malpractice and additional medical board sanctions involves prescribing in a manner that is contraindicated, thereby placing the patient at risk for serious physical harm or death.

These laws are widely known by physicians and it is the job of primary care practitioners like Dr. Sky to understand the standard of care for prescribing medications. In addition, her position as a manager and role in reviewing the work of FBTRHCS primary care physicians gave her a detailed view of the circumstances around which opioids were being prescribed at FBTRHCS. With access to that detailed information about the circumstances of opioid prescriptions at FBTRHCS, both at the global level and in the cases of individual patients, and her knowledge as an experienced physician, Dr. Sky had more than enough information to conclude that FBTRCS's opioid practices violated the laws cited above or similar statutes making this a valid protected disclosure.

b.   Substantial and Specific Danger to Public Health or Safety

Over-prescription of opioids presents a substantial and specific danger to both the patients being unnecessarily prescribed opioids and to the community at large.

Individual patients risk death if given an inappropriate opioid prescription. According to the Centers for Disease Control and Prevention ("CDC") "[f]rom 1999 to 2016, more than 200,000 people have died in the U.S. from overdoses related to prescription opioids." Prescription Opioid Overdose Data, Centers for Disease Control and Prevention, August 1, 2017, available at www.cdc.gov/drugoverdose/data/overdose.html. Further "[o]verdose is not the only risk related to prescription opioids. Misuse, abuse, and opioid use disorder (addiction) are also potential dangers. In 2014, almost 2 million Americans abused or were dependent on prescription opioids." Id. FBTRHCS patients are subject to all of those risks when FBTRHCS physicians over-prescribed opioids and faced a substantial and specific danger as a result.

In addition, however, over-prescription by FBTRHCS physicians not only imperils patients, it endangers the entire surrounding community. Some FBTRHCS patients were diverting opioids to sell in the surrounding community, a fact Dr. Sky was aware of because of the negative urine drug screens she observed.

The illegal sale of prescription opioids creates a serious danger in the surrounding community, leading to increases in opioid addiction, overdoses, and increases in rates of heroin addiction. See e.g. 'Pill Mill' Crackdown Linked to Fewer Painkiller Overdose Deaths in Florida, Johns Hopkins Bloomberg School of Public Health Dec. 21, 2015, available at https://www.jhsph.edu/news/news-releases/2015/pill-mill-crackdown-linked-to-fewer-painkiller-overdose-deaths-in-florida.html. As a physician responsible for prescribing opioids, Dr. Sky was well aware of these dangers to the community.

As an experienced primary care practitioner and manager of physicians with direct knowledge of the patient care of hundreds of patients, Dr. Sky had more than enough knowledge to conclude that over-prescription of opioids presented these dangers both to patients and to the surrounding community, making this a valid protected disclosure.

c.   Gross Mismanagement

These disclosures constitute disclosures under the reasonable belief of gross mismanagement because a reasonable observer would believe that rampant misuse and over prescription of opioids is likely to lead to repeated malpractice claims against the Agency as discussed in subsection (a) directly above.

4.   Supporting Evidence

a.   Sworn Testimony of Dr. Sky. Exhibit G. (declaration)
b.   Context Descriptions of Oral Disclosures. Exhibit H.

d.   Exhibit I, p. 7

A.   Disclosure B: FBTRHCS' Consistent Failure to Properly Interpret Urine Drug Screens

Dr. Sky disclosed to Dr. Chief of Staff that practitioners at the facility were not properly trained in interpreting urine drug screens, and were therefore missing many instances when urine screens were improperly negative. Missing those screens meant that many patients diverting opioids were going undetected (when a drug screen is negative in an opioid patient it means they are not taking the opioids and are likely selling them or otherwise using them inappropriately).

1.   When Was the Disclosure Made?

Fall of 2015, Winter 2015, Spring 2016

2.   To Whom (Name and Title) Was the Disclosure Made?

Dr. Medical Center Chief of Staff

3.   Disclosure of Information Evidenced:

a.   Violation of Law, Rule, or Regulation

See Section IV(A)3(a) above. The failure to properly interpret drug screens leads directly to the potential inappropriate and illegal prescription of opioids because when a patient tests negative for opioids on a urine screen they are very likely diverting opioids.

b.   Substantial and Specific Danger to Public Health or Safety

See Section IV(A)3(b) above and section B(3)(a) directly above. Diversion of opioids for sale in the community leads to the substantial and specific dangers to public health described in Section IV(A)3(b).

c. Gross Mismanagement

See Section IV(A)3(c) above.

4. Supporting Evidence

      a.   Sworn Testimony of Dr. Sky. Exhibit A. (declaration)

C. Disclosure C: Non-Physician Patient Advocates to Improperly Influencing Medical Decisions

Dr. Sky disclosed to Dr. Chief of Staff that FBTRHCS was undermining opioid safety efforts by allowing non-physician patient advocates to improperly influence medical decisions regarding when it was medically safe and necessary to prescribe opioids.

1. When Was Disclosure Made?

      Spring 2016 (Note that the dates are not exhaustive and Dr. Sky disclosed similar incidents verbally on other occasions.)

2. To Whom (Name and Title) Was the Disclosure Made?

      Dr. Medical Center Chief of Staff

3. Disclosure of Information Evidenced:

      a.   Violation of Law, Rule, or Regulation

See Section IV(A)3(a) above. Improper influence on physician medical decisions pressuring those physicians to prescribe opioids when they otherwise would not, in their medical judgement, have done so leads directly to the violations of law described in Section IV(A)3(a) above because those physicians would be prescribing opioids against their medical judgement.

b. Substantial and Specific Danger to Public Health or Safety

See Section IV(A)3(b) above and Section C(3)(a) directly above. Pressuring physicians to prescribe opioids when it would otherwise be against their best medical judgements leads to the substantial and specific dangers to public health described in Section IV(A)3(b) because it pressures physicians to prescribe dangerous opioids despite the overdose and addiction risks to patients and risks of ignoring diversion.

c. Gross Mismanagement

See Section IV(A)3(c) above.

4. Supporting Evidence

a. Sworn testimony of Dr. Sky. Exhibit J.
b. Context Descriptions of Oral Disclosure. Exhibit K.

D. Disclosure D: FBTRHCS's Top Leadership Was Improperly Supporting Non-Physician Patient Advocates in Intervening in Individual Patient Medical Decisions and that Support Was Leading to Unsafe Opioid Prescriptions

Dr. Sky disclosed to Dr. Chief of Staff that patient advocates were inappropriately pressuring physicians to change opioid safety plans and the volume of opioids dispensed to patients, creating pressure on physicians to prescribe opioids inappropriately and endanger both the safety of those patient and the surrounding community. She disclosed that FBTRHCS administration's support of the patient advocates' in disputes about patient opioid prescriptions was leading to inappropriate and unsafe prescriptions against doctors' independent medical judgment.

1.   When Was Disclosure Made?

Spring 2016 (Note that the dates are not exhaustive and Dr. Sky disclosed similar incidents verbally on other occasions.)

2.   To Whom (Name and Title) Was the Disclosure Made?

Dr. Medical Center Chief of Staff

3.   Disclosure of Information Evidenced:

   a.   <u>Violation of Law, Rule, or Regulation</u>

See Section IV(A)3(a) above and Section C(3)(a) above. Improper influence on physician medical decisions pressuring those physicians to prescribe opioids when they otherwise would not, in their medical judgement, have done so leads directly to the violations of law described in Section IV(A)3(a) above because those physicians would be prescribing opioids against their medical judgement.

   b.   <u>Substantial and Specific Danger to Public Health or Safety</u>

See Section IV(A)3(b) above, Section C(3)(a) above, and Section D(3)(a) directly above. Pressuring physicians to prescribe opioids when it would otherwise be against their best medical judgements leads to the substantial and specific dangers to public health described in Section IV(A)3(b) because it pressures physicians to prescribe dangerous opioids despite the overdose and addiction risks to patients and risks of ignoring diversion.

   c.   <u>Gross Mismanagement</u>

See Section IV(A)3(c) above.

4.   Supporting Evidence

    a.   Sworn testimony of Dr. Sky. Exhibit J.
    b.   Context Descriptions of Oral Disclosure. Exhibit K.

E.   Disclosure E: Reporting Patient Diversion of Opioids

Dr. Sky disclosed to Dr. Chief of Staff that patients were diverting opioids prescribed by FBTRHCS physicians and in some cases even selling those diverted opioids on FBTRHCS grounds.

1.   When Was Disclosure Made?

Early summer 2016

2.   To Whom (Name and Title) Was the Disclosure Made?

Dr. Medical Center Chief of Staff

3.   Disclosure of Information Evidenced:

    a.   <u>Violation of Law, Rule, or Regulation</u>

See Section IV(A)3(a) above. The resale of highly controlled opioids on Agency property is a particularly blatant violation of law.

    b.   <u>Substantial and Specific Danger to Public Health or Safety</u>

See Section IV(A)3(b) above. Resale of opioids in the community and on medical center grounds is an obvious threat to public health and safety, as well as the safety of everyone at the medical center.

    c.   <u>Gross Mismanagement</u>

See Section IV(A)3(c) above.

4. Supporting Evidence

    a.   Sworn testimony of Dr. Sky. Exhibit J.

    b.   Context Descriptions of Oral Disclosure. Exhibit K.

F.   Disclosure F: FBTRHCS Unlawfully Pressuring Physicians to Reinstate Opioid Prescriptions Despite those Physicians' Objections

Dr. Sky disclosed to Dr. Chief of Staff that it is unethical and unlawful for the Chief of Staff or other officials to force a physician to write an opioid prescription if the Chief of Staff approved the reinstatement of opioids and the primary care physician is not in agreement. She stated that such coercion is particularly problematic when the primary care physician believes such a prescription is unethical, unlawful, or unsafe for the patient.

1.   When Was Disclosure Made?

Early summer 2016

2.   To Whom (Name and Title) Was the Disclosure Made?

Dr. Medical Center Chief of Staff

3.   Disclosure of Information Evidenced:

    a.   <u>Violation of Law, Rule, or Regulation</u>

See Section IV(A)3(a) above. Improper influence on physician medical decisions pressuring those physicians to prescribe opioids when they otherwise would not, in their medical judgement, have done so leads directly to the violations of law described in Section IV(A)3(a) above because those physicians would be prescribing opioids against their medical judgement. That is particularly true when the physicians believe giving such a prescription would be unsafe for the patient. See, e.g., Exhibit L.

Dr. Sky, as the direct supervisor of the primary care physicians being placed under pressure, was aware of the pressure being placed on them because she reviewed the relevant charts and frequently communicated with her subordinates about opioid prescription renewals and their discussions. In addition, her role as Opioid Safety Initiative Facility Co-Champion gave her additional visibility into these discussions.

b. Substantial and Specific Danger to Public Health or Safety

See Section IV(A)3(b) above and Section F(3)(a) directly above. Pressuring physicians to prescribe opioids when it would otherwise be against their best medical judgements leads the substantial and specific dangers to public health described in Section IV(A)3(b) because it pressures physicians to prescribe dangerous opioids despite the overdose and addiction risks to patients and risks of ignoring diversion.

c. Gross Mismanagement

See Section IV(A)3(c) above.

4. Supporting Evidence

   a. Sworn testimony of Dr. Sky. Exhibit J.
   b. Context Descriptions of Oral Disclosure. Exhibit K.
   c. Example of Dr. CoS forcing physician to prescribe opioids against the physician's medical judgement (*compare* page 1 authorizing early fill of Oxycodone because "Reason: as directed by Dr. CoS" *with* in-depth explanation by Dr. PCP on page 2 describing why prescribing opioids to this patient is dangerous and inappropriate). Exhibit L.

G.   Disclosure G: FBTRHCS Transferring Drug Seeking Patients
to Physicians More Willing to Prescribe Opioids

Dr. Sky disclosed to Dr. Chief of Staff that his decision to relocate a patient from the South Clinic FBTRHCS office to the Other
Clinic FBTRHCS office over the objections of South Clinic's medical staff undermined the moral of the South Clinic staff and created
danger for the particular patient for whom he allowed the transfer.
The South Clinic medical staff had worked to taper that patient off
of opioids and strongly believed that patient only sought a transfer
to a new doctor at Other Clinic in order to keep the patient's current
level of opioid prescriptions in place.

1.   When Was Disclosure Made?

Fall 2016

2.   To Whom (Name and Title) Was the Disclosure Made?

Dr. Medical Center Chief of Staff

3.   Disclosure of Information Evidenced:

a.   Violation of Law, Rule, or Regulation

See Section IV(A)3(a) above. One of the most common tactics
for drug seeking patients who have a physician who refuses to prescribe them more opioids is to go find another physician who will
be more pliable. Physicians are well aware of this practice and by
approving the transfer of patients to other Agency physicians—over
the objections of the staff treating those patients—FBTRHCS management is knowingly enabling patient drug seeking. That creates a
very likely scenario where a patient will receive a prescription without medical need in violation of law and safe medical practice.
   Dr. Sky, as the direct supervisor of all FBTRHCS primary care
physicians, was aware of these transfer requests from FBTRHCS

management and any physician, particularly one with her opioid safety background, would be aware that such transfer requests are classic drug seeking behavior likely to lead to an inappropriate or illegal prescription if that patient is accommodated.

b. Substantial and Specific Danger to Public Health or Safety

See Section IV(A)3(b) above and Section G(3)(a) directly above. Inappropriate transfers of patients among physicians is likely to lead to improper and unsafe prescriptions, creating the dangers described in Section IV(A)3(b) above.

c. Gross Mismanagement

See Section IV(A)3(c) above.

4. Supporting Evidence

   a. Sworn testimony of Dr. Sky. Exhibit J.
   b. Context Descriptions of Oral Disclosure. Exhibit K.

H. Disclosure H: FBTRHCS Overriding Physician Decisions to Taper and Suspend Opioid Prescriptions Endangered Patients

Dr. Sky disclosed to Dr. Chief of Staff that the FBTRHCS administration's increasingly frequent practice of overriding primary care physicians' decisions to taper or suspend opioid prescriptions was endangering the health of patients and obstructing doctors' abilities to treat patients effectively and that it is a breach of legal and ethical obligations to pressure physicians to provide marinol when their initial decision was against providing this controversial drug.

1. When Was Disclosure Made?

Spring 2017

2. To Whom (Name and Title) Was the Disclosure Made?

    Dr. Medical Center Chief of Staff

3. Disclosure of Information Evidenced:

    a. <u>Violation of Law, Rule, or Regulation</u>

See Section IV(A)3(a) above and Section IV(F)3(a) above.

   b. <u>Substantial and Specific Danger to Public Health or Safety</u>

See Section IV(A)3(b) above, Section F(3)(a) above, and Section F(3)(b) above.

    c. <u>Gross Mismanagement</u>

See Section IV(A)3(c) above.

4. Supporting Evidence

    a. Sworn testimony of Dr. Sky. Exhibit J.
    b. Context Descriptions of Oral Disclosure. Exhibit K.
    c. Example of Dr. Chief of Staff improperly interven-
        ing in patient's case to reinstate opioid prescriptions
        to a patient who was a known addict and, prior,
        "shortly after having his narcotic medications tapered,
        intentionally drove his car into a building adjoining
        the clinic." Exhibit M. (Note that Mr. Director was
        included on this email chain, it is highly unusual for
        the director of a medical center to be cc'd on an email
        regarding an individual change in patient care).

I.   Disclosure I: Non-Physician Director Improperly Pressuring Physicians to Prescribe Opioids

Dr. Sky disclosed to Dr. Chief of Staff that Mr. Director was harassing and coercing doctors to provide a prescription to patients after those patients complained about those doctors' medical decisions not to provide opioids (or to reduce opioid levels), and that this action was a breach of law, patient safety, and medical ethics.

1.   When Was Disclosure Made?

Spring 2017 to Dr. Medical Center Chief of Staff

2.   Disclosure of Information Evidenced:

a.   Violation of Law, Rule, or Regulation

See Section IV(A)3(a) above and Section IV(F)3(a) above. It is particularly inappropriate and dangerous for a non-physician like Mr. Director to override the decisions of physicians in the sensitive area of opioid prescription because he lacks any medical training. His intervention makes it especially likely that FBTRHCS would prescribe opioids in violation of law and safe medical practices because of his lack of the requisite training coupled with the power of his office over his physician employees.

b.   Substantial and Specific Danger to Public Health or Safety

See Section IV(A)3(b) above, Section F(3)(a) above, and Section F(3)(b) above.

c.   Gross Mismanagement

See Section IV(A)3(c) above.

3. Supporting Evidence

    a.   Sworn testimony of Dr. Sky. Exhibit J.
    b.   Context Descriptions of Oral Disclosure. Exhibit K.

V.   LIST OF THE AGENCY'S RETALIATORY ACTIONS

1.   New Year 2017 (Leadership Day) and Spring 2017 (staff meeting): Mr. Director subjected Dr. Sky to public ridicule in a number of staff meetings and public events.

    A.   Supporting Evidence

        a.   Sworn testimony of Dr. Sky. Exhibit J.

    B.   Prohibited Personnel Practice

        a.   Significant change in duties, responsibilities, or working conditions

           A hostile work environment, including public ridicule, is sufficient to establish a significant change in duties, responsibilities, or working conditions. *See* discussion of <u>Savage v. Dep't of the Army</u> in Section V(1)(B)(a) below.

2.   Early summer 2017: Agency Released Dr. Sky's photograph and personal information to News Station and held Dr. Sky up as a scapegoat for facility policies. The Medical Center released Dr. Sky's photograph without her permission and Dr. Sky did not participate or wish to participate in the story, nor is she a spokesman for the Agency in any capacity. In addition, this action exposed Dr. Sky to physical danger by holding her up as the individual "to blame" for dozens of potentially addicted patients who had or would have their prescriptions suspended or tapered.

A. Supporting Evidence

    a. Sworn testimony of Dr. Sky. Exhibit J.
    b. Link to video of NEWS Early Summer 2017 news story: http:/news-investigates hospital-in-city-abruptly-cutting-opiate-prescriptions/
    c. Link to story describing doctor in nearby community being killed by an angry patient for not prescribing opioids: https://www.statnews.com/2017/08/08/-doctor-murdered-opioids/
    d. Example of patients threatening FBTRHCS staff over opioid prescriptions. Exhibit N.

B. Prohibited Personnel Practice

    a. Significant Change in Duties, Responsibilities, or Working Conditions

        Courts define a "significant change in duties, responsibilities, or working conditions" prohibited personnel practice broadly and have included a variety of different agency actions within its definition. 5 U.S.C. § 2302(a)(2)(A)(xii). The Board, for example, recently stated in Savage v. Dep't of the Army that:

        "The legislative history of the 1994 amendment to the WPA indicates that the term 'any other significant change in duties, responsibilities, or working conditions' should be interpreted broadly, to include 'any harassment or discrimination that could have a chilling effect on whistleblowing or otherwise undermine the merit system.'"

47

Savage v. Dep't of the Army, 122 M.S.P.R. 612 (MSPB 2015) (a hostile work environment, standing alone, is a "significant change in duties, responsibilities, or working conditions").

A variety of federal circuit courts have reached similarly broad conclusions. For example, the Ninth Circuit found "Congress *did* expect 'prohibited personnel practices' to cover supervisors' violations of employees' constitutional and privacy rights," and consequently "[Plaintiff] could have redressed the alleged defamations and inflictions of emotional distress either by initiating an OSC investigation of prohibited personnel practices..." Saul v. U.S., 928 F.2d 829 (9th Cir.1991) (opening an employee's mail was a "personnel action") (emphasis added).

The Third Circuit found that 2302(a)(2)(A)(xii) encompasses any violations that "occurred only as a result of the employment relationship" and even included actions taken against an employee *after* that employee's termination. Yu v. U.S. Dep't of, No. 11-3165, (3rd Cir., June 4, 2013) (NP) *quoting* Lombardi v. Small Bus. Admin., 889 F.2d 959 (10th Cir. 1989).

The D.C. Circuit held that working conditions under 2302(a)(2)(A)(xii) should be read broadly to include even actions that simply "interfered with [Plaintiff's] decisional independence" because such decisional independence was a part of Plaintiff's working conditions. Mahoney v. Donovan, 721 F.3d 633 (D.C. Cir., 2013).

In the instant case, Mr. Director and Dr. Chief of Staff's actions in releasing Dr. Sky's picture to a local news channel without her consent, consenting to NEWS reporters contacting her without her permission, and holding her up as a public scapegoat for Agency policies constituted a "significant change in duties, responsibilities, or working conditions" under 2302(a)(2)(A)(xii).

First, as in Saul, the Agency releasing Dr. Sky's picture without permission explicitly for use in a public news program constituted a violation of Dr. Sky's privacy and subjected her to both defamation and intense emotional distress. Dr. Chief of Staff's false attacks on the program also subjected her to defamation and intense emotional distress, as did suddenly finding herself as the "target" for hundreds of potentially opioid addicted patients.

Second, as in Yu and Lombardi, the Agency's actions "occurred only as a result of the employment relationship" because the Agency's actions and comments solely concerned Dr. Sky's work as the FBTRHCS Associate Chief of Staff of Primary Care.

Third, as in Mahoney, the Agency's actions devastated Dr. Sky's ability to make independent medical judgements was directly under attack because very few employees would continue to state their honest opinions after such intense and public attacks from their Agency. Those public statements attacking her also severely undermined her leadership authority at the Agency, significantly impairing her ability to act as a manager and coordinator between departments.

Finally, as in Savage, such actions constitute the creation of a hostile work environment because of the intense public embarrassment and physical danger the Agency's actions created for Dr. Sky.

Therefore, the Agency's actions in releasing Dr. Sky's picture to a local news channel without her consent, consenting to News station reporters contacting her without her permission, and holding her up as a public scapegoat for Agency policies constituted a "significant change in duties, responsibilities, or working conditions" under 5 U.S.C. § 2302(a)(2)(A)(xii) and a valid prohibited personnel practice under jurisdiction.

3.   Early Summer 2017: Agency Dr. Chief of Staff attacks Dr. Sky on NEWS Station without a basis in fact and held Dr. Sky up as a scapegoat for facility policies.

   A.   Supporting Evidence

      a.   Sworn testimony of Dr. Sky. Exhibit J.
      b.   Link to video of NEWs Early Summer 2017 news story: http:/news.com/NEWS-investigates-hospital-in-city-abruptly-cutting-opiate-prescriptions/

   B.   Prohibited Personnel Practice

      a.   Significant Change in Duties, Responsibilities, or Working Conditions

See Section V(1)(B)(a) above.

4. Early Summer 2017: The Agency consented to NEWS Station contacting Dr. Sky, adding a new press relations role to her position that was not part of her duties.

    A. Supporting Evidence

        a. Sworn testimony of Dr. Sky. Exhibit J.

    B. Prohibited Personnel Practice

        a. Significant Change in Duties, Responsibilities, or Working Conditions

See Section V(1)(B)(a) above.

5. Early Summer 2017: The Agency issued a Suspension of Privileges against Dr. Sky without following the procedure for doing so outlined in policy or FBTRHCS Medical Staff Bylaws.

    A. Supporting Evidence

        a. Sworn testimony of Dr. Sky. Exhibit J.
        b. Suspension of Privileges. Exhibit D.

    B. Prohibited Personnel Practice

        a. Action Under Chapter 75 of this Title or Other Disciplinary or Corrective Action

            Suspending Dr. Sky's privileges constitutes a disciplinary or corrective action because it is a form of suspension and because its stated purpose was to remedy a past violation of Agency procedures and prevent future violations. *See* 5 C.F.R. § 2635.102. In addition, the removal of medical privileges nearly inevitably leads to the termination of a physician from her position because it renders her unable to perform her basic duties.

b. Significant Change in Duties, Responsibilities, or Working Conditions

Alternatively, the suspension of Dr. Sky's medical privileges constitutes a significant change in her duties, responsibilities or working conditions, because the action removed her ability to work as a physician at FBTRHCS. During her suspension she was no longer allowed to provide patient care or oversee physicians (the core elements of her position) and was temporarily placed in an administrative position.

6. Early Summer 2017: Dr. Sky was removed from her position as Opioid Safety Initiative Facility Co-Champion.

A. Supporting Evidence

a. Sworn testimony of Dr. Sky. Exhibit J.

B. Prohibited Personnel Practice

a. Significant Change in Duties, Responsibilities, or Working Conditions

Overseeing opioid practices throughout FBTRHCS, beyond the scope of primary care alone, was her duty as Opioid Safety Initiative Facility Co-Champion and such duty was removed when the Agency removed her from that position.

7.	Summer 2017: Another candidate is hired for Medical Director at the East Coast Medical Center.

    A.	Supporting Evidence

        a.	Sworn testimony of Dr. Sky. Exhibit J.
        b.	On early summer 2017 Dr. Sky interviewed for the position of Medical Director for Community Services, a new position, at East Coast Medical Center. Dr. Sky was invited for a site visit. Dr. Sky supplied references which were checked. From Early summer 2017 to one week after early summer 2017 Dr. Sky visited the East Coast Medical Center. She received a job offer for the position with a start date of Summer 2017. Dr. Sky put an offer in on a home and it is accepted pending an official final offer from East Coast Medical Center. Following the Early summer 2017 NEWS Station story described above, the official final offer for the position was not made.

    B.	Prohibited Personnel Practice

        a.	Failure to Appoint

        The failure to make an appointment is a prohibited personnel practice. Here, the East Coast office of the Agency rescinded an offered appointment solely because of the public blame placed on Dr. Sky by the Agency.

8.	Summer 2017: Refusal of Mr. Director to sign for reinstatement of Dr. Sky's privileges following a unanimous recommendation for reinstatement by the Professional Standards Board and

Clinical Executive Board on mid-summer 2017. Mr. Director only reinstated Dr. Sky's privileges in late summer 2017.

A. Supporting Evidence

    a. Sworn testimony of Dr. Sky. Exhibit J.

    b. Summer 2017 Email from Dr. Chief of Staff. Exhibit P. (stating that Mr. Director ordered him not to follow the Professional Standards Board's recommendation to restore Dr. Sky's medical privileges).

    c. Late summer 2017 Email Recapping Professional Standards Board Meeting. Exhibit F ("PSB Members request a report from COS to PSB regarding outcome of PSB recommendations from the mid-summer 2017 emergency meeting regarding lifting of summary suspension of Primary Care Service Chief and restoration of ACOS responsibilities.").

    d. Later summer 2017 Email Announcing Full Restoration of Privileges. Exhibit Q.

B. Prohibited Personnel Practice

    a. Action Under Chapter 75 of this Title or Other Disciplinary or Corrective Action

        See Section V(5)(B)(a) above. This action constitutes an extension of the suspension discussed in such subsection.

    b. Significant Change in Duties, Responsibilities, or Working Conditions

See Section V(5)(B)(a) above.

9. Late summer 2017: Dr. CoS at the direction of Mr. Director issues a Proposed Reprimand against Dr. Sky for failure to follow a medical center policy even though the issues forming the basis of the Proposed Reprimand were discussed by the Professional Standards Board and Clinical Executive Board on mid-summer 2017 and found to be meritless.

    A. Supporting Evidence

        a. Sworn testimony of Dr. Sky. Exhibit J.
        b. Proposed Reprimand of Dr. Sky. Exhibit H.

    B. Prohibited Personnel Practice

        a. Action Under Chapter 75 of this Title or Other Disciplinary or Corrective Action

            A formally proposed reprimand is a disciplinary or corrective action.

10. Dr. Sky resigned from the large health care system in the fall of 2017, such resignation constituting an involuntary resignation.

    A. Supporting Evidence

        a. Sworn testimony of Dr. Sky. Exhibit J.
        b. Dr. Sky retired from the organization in the late fall of 2017 in the face of Mr. Director's and Dr. Chief of Staffs' threats against her medical license, unsupported disciplinary actions, and pressure following her disclosures to approve illegal activities that would have subjected her to civil and criminal penalties as described throughout this brief.
        c. Dr. Sky is not the only FBTRHCS primary care physician to resign during this period. Dr.

PCP1, Dr. PCP2, Dr. PCP3, and PCP4, NP, all resigned or otherwise left their positions due to the pressure to prescribe opioids inappropriately that Dr. Sky objected to in her disclosures to the Agency.

B.   Prohibited Personnel Practice

a.   Action Under Chapter 75 of this Title or Other Disciplinary or Corrective Action

An "appellant may pursue an involuntary resignation / retirement claim as a personnel action in an IRA appeal." Mastrullo v. Dept. of Labor, 123 MSPR 110 (MSPB 2015). "One way to overcome the presumption of voluntariness of a resignation is to show that the employee's working conditions were so difficult that a reasonable person in the employee's position would have felt compelled to resign." Glenn v. Soldiers' & Airmen's Home, 76 MSPR 572 (1997).

Dr. Sky was subjected to intense retaliation by the Agency as discussed herein as well as pressure to approve the illegal prescription of opioids. Dr. Sky faced a choice between: 1) staying in her position where she would continue to face intense retaliation, threats to her medical license, public humiliation, physical danger from angry patients, and constant pressure to approve the illegal and unsafe prescription of opioids (subjecting her to a plethora of civil and criminal consequences), and 2) resigning. No one reasonable person would stay in her position under those circumstances.

In addition, resignation by others under similar circumstances is strong evidence that a reasonable person would have resigned. At least four medical practitioners resigned while facing only a portion of the pressure experienced by Dr. Sky, strongly suggesting that a reasonable person would have resigned in her circumstances.

For the foregoing reasons, jurisdiction over Dr. Sky's involuntary resignation is proper as a component of her IRA appeal.

VI. WHY DR. SKY'S DISCLOSURES WERE A CONTRIBUTING FACTOR TO THE AGENCY'S RETALIATORY ACTIONS

"To satisfy the contributing factor criterion at the jurisdictional stage of an IRA appeal, the appellant only need raise a non-frivolous allegation that the fact or the content of the protected disclosure was one factor that tended to affect the personnel action in any way." Bradley, 123 MSPR 547 (MSPB 2016).

Mr. Medical Center Director and Dr. Chief of Staff retaliated against Dr. Sky because her repeated disclosures of instances in which the Medical Center endangered patients and the community at large by over-prescribing opioids impeded their efforts to pursue high patient satisfaction scores.

Between Dr. Sky's arrival and the spring of 2017, Medical Center physicians began prescribing fewer opioids, which created a backlash among patients whose prescriptions were being tapered or suspended. Exhibit Q (data analytics showing reduction in opioid prescriptions). Patient dissatisfaction with physicians' decisions to taper or suspend their opioid prescriptions created a constant stream of complaints to the patient advocates and drove down measures of patient satisfaction.

The medical center's top officials, Mr. Director and Dr. Chief of Staff, were highly sensitive to public criticism of the facility. In particular, Mr.

Medical Center Director's job evaluations are directly tied to evaluations of patient satisfaction and he frequently emphasizes the importance of patient satisfaction when communicating with Medical Center staff. *see* Exhibit I (critical elements 4 and 5); Exhibit J (sample questions); Exhibit K (discussing Director's focus on patient satisfaction). Dr. Sky also alleges under information and belief that Mr. Director and Dr. Chief of Staffs' bonuses are tied in part to the Medical Center's patient satisfaction ratings.

The backlash against tighter opioid controls manifested in part as a concerted campaign by a few patients against the medical center's opioid reductions, including heavy use of the medical center's patient advocate system, calls to medical center officials, lobbying members of Congress to intervene, and contacting the news media. *See e.g.*, NEWS Investigates Hospital In City Abruptly Cutting Opiate Prescriptions, NEWS Spring 2017 *available at* http://NEWS.com/2017/05/NEWS-investigates-hospital-in-city-abruptly-cutting-opiate-prescriptions/. These patient protesters' central charge was that doctors were not always meeting with patients before tapering or suspending their opioid prescriptions and they seized on a misinterpretation of a State Medical Board standard to argue that this practice was inappropriate.

After Dr. Sky's disclosures and conversations with him about opioids, Mr. Director frequently stated that he "supports the patients" meaning that when patient satisfaction and opioid safety collided, he gave patients the benefit of the doubt despite the serious safety and legal concerns raised by Dr. Sky. It also shows his clear disagreement with her disclosures and suggests an ad hominem approach to the issue (i.e., his statements strongly implied he believed Dr. Sky does *not* support patients when she raised medical concerns about treatment).

The retaliation against Dr. Sky detailed above follows closely in time after the early spring 2017 NEWS local news story discussing the dissatisfied patients' complaints. Days after the local news story aired, the medical center director issued an emergency suspension of privileges three days later in the early spring 2017. That close connection in time shows the two events were intimately connected. Moreover, that suspension of privileges did not follow either the policy or FBTRHCS Medical Staff Bylaws, which also shows that the suspension was retaliatory in nature rather than a proper disciplinary practice.

Further, FBTRHCS's Professional Standards Board and Clinical Executive Board undertook an investigation of the charges against Dr. Sky that supposedly required an emergency suspension. They found the underlying charges to be meritless, recommending Dr. Sky's reinstatement. Exhibit F. Mr. Director however, initially refused to implement the decision of the boards despite him not being a medical practitioner and not having any clinical expertise, clearly showing a retaliatory motive against Dr. Sky rather than a concern for patient safety or Medical Center policy. *See* Exhibit E; Exhibit F. He only relented and signed the reinstatement of her privileges 11 days later when he realized he had no lawful grounds for withholding them.

Subsequently, the medical center retaliated against Dr. Sky again by issuing a Proposed Reprimand for the same issues it had attempted to suspend her privileges for. Exhibit H. This second attempt to discipline Dr. Sky is both an act of retaliation in and of itself, and evidence showing a retaliatory motive because the underlying policies at issue had already been discussed in the prior forum of the Professional Standards Board. Attempting to discipline Dr. Sky for a medical practice that the facility's own medical standards boards had found to be proper clearly has no basis in legitimate disciplinary motives.

There is no doubt that these actions were tied directly to Dr. Sky's disclosures on improper opioid practices because the discipline proposed against her was for implementing the tougher opioid practices she called for in her disclosures and, as discussed above, followed just days after negative publicity about tougher opioid practices championed by Dr. Sky. In addition, the Agency's decision to discuss Dr. Sky personally in the NEWS Station story, even going so far as to distribute her picture without her permission, shows Mr. Director and Dr. Chief of Staff's clear intent to deflect blame on Dr. Sky personally.

Further, the underlying charges in both the suspension of privileges and Proposed Reprimand themselves show an improper retaliatory motive for the reasons set forth below:

> First, FBTRHCS has routinely allowed changes to be made to patient opioid prescriptions in supposed violation of State Medical Board rules as they now interpret them. In particular, between the time when the rule was first issued in November 2014 and Dr. Sky's hiring in the fall of 2015, FBTRHCS routinely allowed patient opioid prescriptions to be changed without the meetings they now say State Medical Board rules require. Before Dr. Sky's hiring, Dr. CoS himself oversaw these routine practices but neither he nor any other employees were disciplined. FBTRHCS never cared about these practices until they became a convenient way to blame Dr. Sky, clearly showing retaliation.

> Second, FBTRHCS has previously interpreted the State Medical Board opioid rule differently than it did in its discipline against Dr. Sky. In communications to physicians, Dr. CoS explicitly stated that it was ok to make changes to opioid prescriptions even if the supposedly required meetings had not occurred. That sudden change in interpretation clearly shows retaliatory motive because the change was made without examination or explanation. And even, for the sake of argument, if the change in interpretation was an honest one then such an honest change of policy would mean that

Dr. Sky should not have been punished—she was just following the then-current policy.

Third, the Medical Center's interpretation of the State Medical Board's opioid rule is clearly an incorrect reading of the rule because *under the interpretation put forward by* FBTRHCS *in its actions against Dr. Sky, any patient who has been prescribed opioids could secure permanent renewals of those prescriptions simply by avoiding a meeting with their physician.* Such an interpretation is false on its face (particularly in light of the strict state, federal, and licensure laws discussed above tightly regulating prescription of opioids, including criminal statutes) and using that clearly incorrect position as the basis for discipline shows the agency's intent was to punish Dr. Sky.

Fourth, it is important to note that Dr. Sky did as much as practically possible to ensure patients were consulted before a change to their opioid prescriptions was made. Specifically, all patients were contacted by FBTRHCS and offered in person appointments to discuss a potential taper or suspension in their opioid prescriptions. The patients who did not have those meetings could have done so had they chosen to.

In sum, Dr. Sky's repeated disclosures regarding FBTRHCS's opioid practices were clearly linked to the Agency's retaliatory actions because each one of those retaliatory actions directly attacked Dr. Sky for advocating medically sound opioid practices—the precise issues focused on in her disclosures. Further, that retaliation began soon after close public scrutiny of FBTRHCS opioid practices; releasing Dr. Sky's picture and blaming her personally in the media followed no Agency procedures or policies and served no conceivable disciplinary or policy goals; Mr. Director's suspension of Dr. Sky's medical privileges did not follow procedures and was not tied to any violation of Agency rules; after Dr. Sky was cleared of that suspension, Mr. Director refused to follow the FBTRHCS Professional Standards Board's decision and subsequently proposed a reprimand on the same issues Dr. Sky was cleared by the Professional Standards Board; and both formal disciplinary actions against Dr. Sky were based on shifting explanations, inconsistent application of discipline, and clearly wrong interpretations of medical standards that stand directly at odds with the stringent legal standards surrounding prescription of opioids.

Those intense inconsistencies combined with the Agency's actions against Dr. Sky all being explicitly based on her advocacy of medically required stringent opioid practices clearly show that her opioid disclosures were a contributing factor to the Agency's retaliatory actions.

I.   CONCLUSION

For the reasons outlined above Dr. Sky respectfully requests that the judge accept jurisdiction over all claims, disclosures, acts of retaliation, and arguments presented herein.

> I have fought a good fight, I have finished my
> course, I have kept the faith.
> —2 Timothy 4:7 (KJV)

CHAPTER 3

Interrogatory Preparation

> For the kingdom of heaven is like unto a man
> that is an householder, which went out early in
> the morning to hire laborers into his vineyard...
> They say unto him, because no man hath hired
> us. He saith unto them, Go ye also into the vine-
> yard; and whatsoever is right, that shall ye receive.
> —Matthew 20:1–16 (KJV, abbreviated)

I earned the privilege to assist my attorney in preparation for the Legal Battle Board hearing. I labored and prepared multiple lists to help in the preparation of my case and decrease legal preparation fees. Fortunately, my attorney and I worked well together and my efforts were appreciated. At one point, another attorney was assigned to help us prepare our case, but we did not jive at all and he only cost me more time and money. I essentially did all of the preparation only to have him give me more assignments. We dropped him from the case and his fees were waived. I appreciated the fairness of the firm and my attorney. My attorney and I pressed on, laboring over our tasks at hand, as a dynamic duo.

My first list consisted of documents to consider requesting from the agency. Opioid Safety Workgroup agendas and minutes first came to mind. Dr. Chief of Staff rarely attended the meetings and this would become quite evident by attendance records. It would be easy to see that I led most of the meetings and that the group engaged in making safety changes at our facility. The attendance records also provided a list of clinical staff to interview. The dates requested encompassed the new year of 2015 to the present to review what occurred before, during, and after my arrival in the late fall of 2015.

I included notes stating it should be evident that Dr. Chief of staff failed to lead the group and that the primary care team accomplished most of the work assignments. In addition to the workgroup requested information, agendas and minutes from Primary Care Medical Home Steering Committee, Primary Care Operations Committee, and Primary Care Provider Meetings were under consideration for review. In combination, all of these groups documented meetings and educational efforts in multiple venues to help reach out to employees, patients, facility leaders, and politicians in an organized fashion to inform others of our efforts to provide safe quality healthcare to our patients.

Requesting Patient Advocate Tracking System records for primary care painted the grim picture of what we as a primary care group were up against. If patients expressed dissatisfaction in any way, they had multiple avenues to complain beginning with visiting patient advocates. The advocates' duties entailed listening to patients and documentation of the complaints into the tracking system. From there, the advocates contacted the primary care leadership team to investigate the complaint. The administrative officer for primary care would review the patient record, reach out to the patient and the primary care team, and problem solve. The encounters would be documented in the tracking system along with the satisfactory resolution of the complaint to the parties involved. This process worked well for many types of complaints; but when opioid safety initiatives became imperative, the process often came to a screeching halt.

Many chronic pain patients understood our efforts to prevent unintentional overdoses and death. When the provider explained why medication doses needed to be reduced while offering alternatives to treat pain, they engaged. Our facility began offering chiropractic care, acupuncture, specialty pain treatments, pain control devices (which were not cheap), pain psychology and counseling, music therapy, mindfulness, and more. We contracted with specialists outside of our facility and smoothed rough processes and procedures in order to expedite care. These efforts proved to be exhausting but well worth our time and effort.

To our dismay but not surprise, we failed to make all of our patients happy. The reasons were beyond our control and actually beyond our imagination. Patients educated us…continuously. Patients flooded the patient advocate offices. The advocates in turn would show up at the primary care department during clinic time, knock on the providers' clinic doors, interrupting scheduled appointments. The advocates expected providers to drop what they were doing to address the advocates' requests immediately. This practice by the advocates infuriated primary care providers. Essentially, the advocates failed to respect the scheduled patients' appointments by interrupting. The advocates expected the providers to immediately resolve the request, failing to realize that clinical reviews would be needed and this would take time. I stopped this practice by the advocates immediately. However, I instantly became their adversary as the roadblock to resolving their complaints immediately. Often, the complaining patients were accompanying the advocates or waiting impatiently in the advocates' offices for a refill of their medication immediately. Now, the advocates needed to actually put their training and expertise to work with finesse to appease the patients or at least coax them into applying some restraint and patience in the process of addressing their complaints. The advocates lacked finesse. In general, some of the advocates over empathized with the patients and one shared later that he battled chronic pain.

Clinical staff educated the patient advocates. We spent over six hours educating the group about opioid safety initiatives over a series of educational meetings. I don't think the advocates heard a word. Instead, the advocates dug their heels in and sided with the complaining patients every time. I cannot think of one encounter in which I was involved where I noticed the light bulb lighting up in their heads. I gave up. I realize this was not my brightest moment; but I had enough and there was nothing left in me to help change this situation. The primary care administrative officers continued to work with the advocates and I was grateful. We all met as a group with the chief of staff to try to bring resolution when faced with impasses; but the chief of staff failed miserably as a negotiator. The patient advocate group grew to become a monstrous sliver in our sides and later planks in our eyes. We encountered an impasse and this group had power, much to my ignorance and surprise.

As I worked with my attorney, I suggested requesting patient drug seeking and opioid safety flag lists in addition to the advocate tracking logs. I placed seventy-two flags on patients' charts within the first few months of my arrival. There were over 350 safety flags on patients' charts for the facility in relation to opioid safety in general. The purpose and practice of placing flags on charts came to fruition as a means to alert clinical staff to safety concerns about patients. A message popped up when a clinician opened the medical record. As the medical community became more transparent and allowed patients to access their records, the patients saw the messages and many of them complained. These complaints added to the burden of the advocates' jobs and soon the complaints escalated landing on the desks of the chief of staff, director, and politicians. Our challenges exponentially increased.

The facility tracked complaints at multiple locations. As previously mentioned, locations included: patient advocate tracking system, primary care and other specialty offices, chief of staff office, director's office, and political tracking system. The primary care administrative officers fielded complaints thrown at them from multiple locations and often the same complaint came around repeatedly. The administrative officers juggled grievances continuously. They reluctantly earned the official title of *patient advocate assistants*. Fortunately for me, these administrative officers excelled. They kept me safe. I continually assisted with medical reviews; but they took on the angry patients and angry advocates head on. Additionally, they recognized and understood the ignorance of the advocates which validated my thoughts and frustrations.

I suggested requesting the clinical medical reviews related to my summary suspension. An internal and external medical review took place. I received a copy of the internal review by the quality management nursing staff. I heard about an external review by professionals outside of our facility; but I still have not seen this report. I learned

I faired extremely well. Well, I had to have done well because Mr. Director eventually reinstated my clinical privileges and this must have tortured him.

Requests for the Ignorant Oversight Body (IOB) documents, Accountability Office to the IOB, and return visit transcripts would be helpful in uncovering lies told by senior officials. I personally knew the chief of staff lied under oath about multiple topics and for what reason I could not fathom. Most of the time there was no reason to lie. Lying simply came easy to him. The chief of staff's vocabulary list is second to none and his politically savvy monologue would have impressed me if the content proved truthful. I wondered who else lied and why.

I suggested requesting Administrative Board transcripts and reports containing interviews by the same employees during the same timeframe that the Ignorant Oversight Body interviewed employees. Their conclusions contradicted one another. In one, I was vindicated. In the other, I deserved punishment. Clinically, I shined twice; but for some reason investigators ignored the clinical review results.

More information to contemplate came in the form of quality management responses to the regional office, presidential inquiries, quality management responses to the Drug Enforcement Agency and internal investigators. May I remind you that my primary care officers and I prepared all of the facility's responses to each of these groups? Requests for regional and national pain management committee agendas, graphs, and minutes would show the efforts required by the organization to address opioid safety. I was not the sole initiator of this important effort. Couldn't anyone see that I did not operate alone?

My attorney requested a list of employees for friendly interviews. I prepared the list effortlessly. Originally, I listed all of the primary care, acute medicine, pharmacy, social work, mental health, chaplain, quality management, systems redesign, police, and other staff including leaders. I found comfort in the realization that employees supported me and our efforts as a team. There proved to be too many to list or even think of interviewing. We narrowed the interviews down to a select few in the end.

In addition to friendly interviews, my attorney requested not so friendly interview names. In reality, the not so friendly were other chiefs who knew the truth, but their jobs depended on loyalty to the director. They witnessed my plight and did not desire the same unsolicited attention. I pondered this list carefully. In the end, I eliminated the devoted chiefs and listed the obvious foes. Most of the list consisted of the director's good old boys, young comrades he could control, and surprisingly dishonest leaders such as the human resources chief (which I realized later after reviewing transcripts).

Miscellaneous requests included: newspaper articles, arrested patient articles, list of patients who overdosed, Dr. Chief of Staff activities with chronic pain patients, and patient chart requests. The medical chart requests consisted of: patients with inappropriately negative urine drug screens (there was no drug in the urine and there should have been drug in the urine), convicted or charged patients related to opioids, patients in which Mr. Director became involved, patients involved with political inquiries, addicted patients, patients found to be double dipping (filling opioid prescriptions at multiple locations), and patients who overdosed on their opioid medication.

Lastly, I put together a list of handbooks, directives, policies, guidelines, roadmaps, legal documents, and other references related to our case. The list encompassed two full pages. Our case stood on solid ground.

CHAPTER 4
Endless Interrogatories

Now he that planteth and he that watereth are
one: and every man shall receive his own reward
according to his own labour. For we are labourers
together with God: ye are God's husbandry, ye
are God's building.
—1 Corinthians 3:8–9 (KJV)

The facility submitted interrogatory requests and documentation
requests also. The agency asked me to: describe in detail the alleged
public ridicule on leadership day and at the meeting in the spring
of 2017; list my employment history, list my employment applications from 2015 to the present; list current salary, bonuses, incentives, relocation income; identify remedies and facts about any claims
I intended to make for equitable relief; identify all attorney's fees
in connection with this appeal; identify costs associated with this
appeal; identify every person I intended to call as a witness; identify
any notes, diaries, or other written documents related to allegations
forming the basis of my appeal; identify too many to list requests
related to reference materials, federal statutes, persons with personal
knowledge of the facts related to reprisal for whistleblowing activity;
identify any complaints or grievances to other parties; explain why
I expected to be hired by East Coast Medical Center and how my
whistleblowing activity caused another individual to be hired; identify persons I consulted to complete the interrogatories and persons
with knowledge of my claimed damages.

Documents requested consisted of: my official personnel file (which they possess); copies of documents relating to answering interrogatories; documents identified in answering the facility's interrogatories; documents of communication to facility management officials; documents to the Complaint Department Office; documents related to my work in opioid safety; documents of correspondence to East Coast Medical Center; copies of all letters, emails, text messages, and other communication related to my allegations; copies of attorney's fees; copies of documents relating to any claims of damages and non-pecuniary compensatory damages, lost pay or leave; lists for any expert witnesses to be at the hearing; copies of notes, diaries, journals, letters, texts, emails, calendars, social media posts related to my allegations of whistleblowing; evidence of current salary, wages, bonuses, benefits received from my current employer.

Our request and the facility's request letter were of equal length. I don't know why this struck me as funny. I guess I wanted a fair fight and having twenty pages of requested items by both parties squared off both sides equally. Of course, the content of the requests varied considerably. The facility requested documents they had complete access to already and to ask us for copies was simply an exercise in wasting our time and my money, a tactic often played by organizations with deep pockets. In reality, it was not a fair fight. I was simply trying to fool myself into thinking I could win this battle. But wait, I forgot what and who was in control…truth and God!

My next assignment entailed the laborious task of answering the endless facility interrogatories. The first interrogatory asked me to describe the public ridicule I endured on a specific leadership day. Following is my reply:

Leadership Day Meeting: Early New Year 2017

I endured thirty to forty-five minutes of ridicule, harassment and personal humiliation from angry patients while Mr. Director, stood by and smiled. I endured personal humiliation from an angry patient for thirty to forty-five minutes in front of my peers.

One patient was upset that his compensation and pension out-come was not as he wanted and he directed his comments at Ms. Administrative Officer to the Deputy Chief of Staff and leader of Compensation and Pension. Mr. Director allowed this patient to direct angry comments to the group focusing on her while Mr. Director stood up front as the host and smiled.

Another patient identified me publicly and complained about opioids and how I was responsible for his pain and suffering while Mr. Director stood up front as the host and smiled.

About seventy-five to one hundred leaders from all the depart-ments attended the training session; I was sitting up in front of the auditorium so it is difficult to list all who were present.

> Mr. Director said nothing to the patients while they humiliated Ms. Administrative Officer and me. He let them talk until they were finished. The patient speaking about Compensation and Pension acknowledged that he should stop and looked to Mr. Director to see if he could continue and Mr. Director gave him a nod to continue. I cannot recall if Mr. Director spoke or not. The patient did continue. I was concerned about how Ms. Administrative Officer felt at the time.

The patients spoke for about thirty to forty-five minutes each and eventually they started to repeat themselves realizing it was time to stop. They vented directly at the two of us.

I expected Mr. Director to remind the patients to be respectful and not use names or titles. I expected Mr. Director to interrupt the patients when they singled out leaders in the audience. When the patients looked to him about time limitations, Mr. Director should have taken the opportunity to thank the patient and move onto the next guest.

As leaders attending an educational meeting, the director informed us that the patients wanted to let us know how we were doing as a facility, the good and the bad, so we can improve our customer service. This was not a town hall setting. This was Leadership Development Day, a learning environment.

Mr. HR Chief spoke to Mr. Director immediately after the meeting and told him the meeting was inappropriate. Mr. HR Chief informed me of this encounter. I confronted the executive leaders at morning report and told them that I felt harassed at the Leadership Development Day meeting. I told them I was humiliated and that I expected Mr. Director to have intervened to stop the harassment. Mr. Director's administrative officer said the patients were told not to single people out by name or title. I then asked why Mr. Director did not intervene when this occurred? Mr. Director then stated, "I always believe the patients." Beyond this statement, I do not recall what else was said by Mr. Director. I do recall that I said that I did not want to be disrespectful in bringing this up at this time; but I wanted everyone to be aware that I felt embarrassed personally and professionally. I felt harassed. I referred to the value of respect and requested that leaders along with patients be respected. I ended the conversation stating, "I expect Ms. Administrative Officer felt the same way (embarrassed personally, professionally and harassed)."

I met with Dr. Chief of Staff, my supervisor, individually to provide greater detail about my response to the meeting. Dr Chief of Staff stated that the executive leadership team met with Mr. Director about the inappropriateness of the meeting and asked Mr. Director to apologize at the next meeting (a month later). Dr. Chief of Staff said, "Mr. Director is unyielding." I asked for an apology. The next Leadership Development Day came and went. Dr. Chief of Staff was not present. Mr. Director did not apologize. I met with Dr. Chief of Staff, my supervisor, upon his return and informed him that no apology occurred at Leadership Development Day. Ms. Mental Health Chief requested an apology also during a chiefs meeting with Dr. Chief of Staff. I reminded Dr. Chief of Staff of this also. Dr. Chief of Staff said he would meet with Mr. Director. Mr. Director failed to apologize to the leadership group.

Background: When Mr. Director first arrived in the fall of 2016, he asked the leaders what he could do to support us and we went around the table. When my turn came, I asked him to please support opioid safety and the primary care providers. I asked for a meeting with Mr. Director and Dr. Chief of Staff. I ended up speaking to them after a morning report. I had a report to show Mr. Director of my findings regarding opioid safety diversion, doctor shopping, patient overdoses, and patient arrests due to selling their opioids. He did not want to see the report stating, "I will always believe the patients." I explained that we have an opioid epidemic in the United States and not only at our facility. Our patients and community members are overdosing every day and some of our patients are not truthful in what they are doing with their opioid medication so we need to be firm with applying opioid safety initiatives. He stated, "I will always believe the patients." That was the end of the meeting.

Dr. Chief of Staff asked to speak with me alone after the meeting with the director and informed me that all Mr. Director heard was me say was patients are diverting and he was angry. Dr. Chief of Staff said he was not happy that I requested the meeting and I should have discussed this with him. I replied that I always discuss this concern with him and that the new director needed to be informed and educated in order to support the primary care providers. I reminded him that patients will usually complain to the patient advocates, chief of staff office, director's office, and to politicians. Those who were making money most likely feel desperate and will complain to try to get their opioids back to sell. I said I understand their desperation, but we as doctors cannot be suppliers.

Mr. AO to Primary Care began presenting weekly for our service line at morning report. He related how patients using opioids for chronic pain affected our access (the only thing the executive leadership team wanted to hear about was access and this fact was plainly stated by Dr. Chief of Staff). At the end of each PowerPoint report, Mr. AO had a slide asking the leaders to support the primary care providers. (These reports are available if needed.) Mr. Director regularly reminded us at those morning reports that he would "always believe the patients (when they complained)."

The second interrogatory asked me to describe the humiliating meeting led by Mr. Director in front of my peers.

Spring 2017. I replied:

On the spring day in 2017 from 11 AM to 12 PM, a leadership meeting was called at the last moment by Mr. Director. I was sitting with Mr. AO and Dr. Acute Medicine waiting for that meeting to start when I was called out to the hallway by Ms. Administrative Officer to the Director. She informed me that the director was addressing the incident from the news story in which I was the subject and this is the topic of the meeting. I asked Ms. AO if I should not attend and she said "it's up to you." I attended. I walked in after Mr. Director started the meeting. Mr. Director's delivered a very vague speech. He spoke about checking for dust and closet clutter and the audience appeared confused. At one point, Mr. Director said, "this will blow over," and "we need to move ahead." Mr. Director asked for questions and he started talking again just as I was raising my hand. Mr. Director said, "let me finish!" Mr. Director finished his statement and then I addressed Mr. Director. I asked for clarification stating that "you asked for questions and would you please respectfully allow me to ask a question?" I then turned to the group in the audience and asked if the audience would like me to address the elephant in the room (me). My colleagues nodded. I then stated that I did not participate in the news interview because I would've had to say unflattering things about Facility by the River Health Care System and its state (about opioid safety initiatives and loss of primary care providers) prior to my arrival. I also stated that I knew I could not disclose any patient medical information. For both of these reasons, it would've been inappropriate for me to be interviewed. I then thanked everyone for listening and sat down. I felt very embarrassed and humiliated by the harsh tone in which Mr. Director addressed me in front of my colleagues and I'm sure I turned very red. Immediately following the meeting, I went directly to my office.

Soon after I returned my office, Dr. Chaplain arrived to check on me. It was clear to Dr. Chaplain and to me that I was very upset by the meeting topic and the way I was addressed publicly by Mr. Director. Dr. Chaplain gave me his cell number and asked me to call at any time, clearly recognizing the disrespectful and humiliating manner in which Mr. Director addressed me during the meeting.

Shortly after Dr. Chaplain's departure, Dr. Mental Health Provider contacted me. She stated she was concerned about how I was feeling due to the public humiliation by Mr. Director. She stated "he would never talk to a male that way." She offered support.

About three hours later, I received a summary suspension of privileges presented by Dr. Chief of Staff. Dr. Chief of Staff told me that this was ordered by Mr. Director. I asked if the Professional Standards Board was involved. He said no, only him as the chair. I addressed that the process of presenting a summary suspension was to involve the Professional Standards Board and the process required my participation to present my side of the story. Dr. Chief of Staff stated that Mr. Director wanted this (presentation of the summary suspension of my privileges) done today. Dr. Chief of Staff said that he agreed. I asked him why he was changing his story. Dr. Chief of Staff would not initially explain. I informed Dr. Chief of Staff what occurred at the director's meeting that same day at 11 AM and that I was publicly dismissed and treated disrespectfully for the second time in front of a group which included all the services chiefs and leaders. Dr. Chief of Staff stated that he would speak to Mr. Director on Tuesday (Monday was a holiday. This discussion occurred on the Friday prior.) I informed Dr. Chief of Staff that I would need to take formal action. Dr. Chief of Staff said I have the right, but he asked me to wait a week. I reminded him that the director and he as the Chief of Staff gave false hope to Ms. Nurse Practitioner about giving her due process for appeal without even considering her appeal. I explained to him that I was aware that the administrative officers for primary care were told to hire Dr. New PCP (replacing Ms. NP) without waiting for Ms. NP's appeal process to take place. I told Dr. Chief of Staff that I was aware that Mr. Director had no intention of listening to Ms. NP or bringing her back as a provider. I expressed to Dr. Chief of Staff that I was not in agreement as to how the director and he has a Chief of Staff handled these situations. They're very unfair to employees. I expressed that they fail to follow processes. Dr. Chief of Staff said that my situation was different. Dr. Chief of Staff said I didn't do anything wrong and he thought I had a long career at the organization. I asked Dr. Chief of Staff how he could say that with what he was proposing regarding my summary suspension of privileges. I stated to Dr. Chief of Staff that I did not do anything to deserve this and that I was just implementing opioid safety. I said to Dr. Chief of Staff that this was all political just like Ms. NP's case. I showed Dr. Chief of Staff the stack emails that I had been sending to the Ignorant Oversight Body Office of Accountability since the day prior which they had requested. Now, my privileges were being summarily suspended without following proper policies and procedures. The Office of Accountability was still reviewing what I was sending to them. I reviewed with Dr. Chief of Staff that he supported what I was doing as a service leader. I reviewed with Dr. Chief of Staff that I understood that face-to-face visits are best but this cannot always be done and he agreed with me. He stood there dumbfounded. I signed the form.

Interrogatory number three requested my full employment history. I attached a copy of my curriculum vitae.

Dr. B. Sky, M.B.A.   (555) 555-1234
                                      bsky@med.org

Professional

Big Blessing Medical Center   Fall 2017–Present
1 God's Reward Lane
Under the sun, State
555-555-1111
Outpatient Primary Care Provider
40 hours per week

Facility by the River Health Care System   Fall 2015–Fall 2017
666 Devil's Tongue Fork
River City, State
555-555-6666

Associate Chief of Staff, Primary Care;
Facility Opioid Safety Co-champion
40 hours per week minimum
Retired early due to hostile work environment and concern about opioid
safety practices; ongoing litigation

- Primary and Preventive Committee
- Leadership, supervisory, oversight responsibilities of Primary Care Outpatient Clinics, Urgent Care at multiple locations
- Access Facility Champion
- Opioid Safety Facility Champion
- Quality Improvement Participation: Work Group Medication Reconciliation, Workgroup Access, Workgroup for Dermatology
- Chair: Medical Home Steering Committee, Opioid Safety Committee, Medical Home Operations, CME Workgroup
- Membership: Clinical Executive Board, Peer Review Committee, P&T Committee, Quality Executive Board, Professional Standard Board, Telemedicine Committee, Clinical Practice Guidelines Committee
- Coach and Mentor Fellow Certification-active

Land of Corn and Soybeans   Oct 2010–Oct 2015
Health Care System
777 Big Challenges Blvd.
Farmersville, State
555-555-5999
Primary and Specialty Care
Service Line Director
40 hours per week minimum
Supportive Chief of Staff retiring;
sought opportunity at FBTRHCS

- Leadership Training Regional Graduate; Coach and Mentor Fellow Certification
- Leadership, supervisory, oversight responsibilities of the ICU, ED, Inpatient Medical Ward, Primary Care Clinics, Specialty Clinics, Compensation and Pension Departments
- Membership: Clinical Executive Council, Peer Review, Primary Care Executive (Chair), P&T Committee, ICU Governance and Code Blue (Chair), Telemedicine Committee, Medical Home Steering (Chair), more
- NDMS Leader and Participant; Multiple full-scale exercises; Center for Domestic Preparedness Healthcare Leadership for Mass Casualty Incidents 14-15 HCL

Great Lakes Medical Center   Spring 2002–Fall 2010
54 Help Me Circle
Construction, State
555-555-0987
Clinical Manager for Community Clinic
40 hours per week minimum
Offered first job in leadership
after receiving MBA and National
Leadership Training completion;
increase in salary appreciated

- Leadership Training Graduate
- Initiated Tele-dermatology Program, Veteran Therapeutic Horseback Riding Program; Honor Flight Physician for WWII Veterans, Library of Congress Historian

Private General Practice   Fall 1998–Spring 2002
98 Cemetery Run
Tourist, State
40 hours per week minimum

- Establishment of a fully functioning private solo practice for adult and pediatric patients

Closed the practice due to burnout; 24 hour /7days a week on-call; accepted a position at the large health care system without any call as an outpatient physician

Military Family Practice Hospital   Summer 1995–Fall 1998
8765 Icy Hill Drive
Shore, State
40 hours per week minimum
Finished commitment for
Health Professional Scholarship
Program-Honorable Discharge

- General Medical Officer Naval Ambulatory and Primary Care Center / Active Duty/ Lieutenant Commander
- Accomplishments include: Team Leader of Primary Care Center, Co-chair of Family Advocacy Committee of Submarine Base, Spouse Abuse Case Review Committee Chairman, Child Case Review Committee Member, Regional Physician for the Multi-victim Child Sexual Abuse Response Team, Lecturer, Preceptor, Member Wellness and Prevention Quality Management Board, Ethics Committee; Combat Casualty Care Course (C4); Fleet Hospital Training Exercise; Naval Commendation Medal

Interrogatory number four required me to list all of the employment applications I filled out since the fall of 2015. I exported the answer directly from the company website.

Application Exported from the Company Website

Job Title	Pay Plan	Location
Physician—Chief of Staff	aa	Land of Corn and Soybeans
PHYSICIAN—ASSOCIATE CHIEF OF STAFF	aa	Rocky Mountains
Physician—Associate Chief of Staff for Clinical Operations	aa	Land of Pretty Trees
DEPUTY CHIEF OF STAFF (PHYSICIAN)	aa	Big Mountain Place
Associate Chief of Staff, Office of the Director	aa	Lots of Snow Country
Physician (Associate Chief of Staff for Primary Care)	aa	By the River
Physician, Associate Chief of Staff (ACOS) Primary Care	aa	White Water Rafting Paradise
Physician (Chief, Medical Service)	aa	Great Boots and Music
Physician (Assistant Chief, Medical Service)	aa	Great Boots and Music
Physician (Chief of Staff)	aa	Summer Paradise

Physician (Deputy, Chief of Staff)	aa	Great Boots and Music
Physician (Chief of Primary Care)	aa	Dry Lands
Physician (Chief Primary Care) Amended Closing Date	aa	Reese's Knockoff
Physician—Chief of Staff	aa	Soybeans and Corn Land of Power Struggles
Medical Officer (Administration)	aa	Location Negotiable After Selection, United States
Physician (Internist/Family Medicine/Physical Medicine & Rehabilitation)	aa	Great Lakes
Chief of Staff (Physician)	aa	Too Close to the River State
Staff Physician (Chief of Quality, Safety & Value Service)	aa	Too Close to the River State 2
Associate Chief of Staff for Ambulatory Care—Physician	aa	Christmas Paradise

Associate Chief of Staff for Education—Physician	aa	Too Blue State
PHYSICIAN (MEDICAL DIRECTOR—COMMUNITY a CLINICS)	aa	Shore town
Physician (Deputy Chief of Staff)	aa	Humid Place
Physician (Clinical Director)	aa	Horse Country
Physician (Chief of Primary Care)	aa	History State
Supervisory Medical Officer (Clinical Director)	aa	Barren, State
Physician (Section Chief, Primary Care)	aa	Oceans of Sunshine
Primary Care Physician (Medical Home Team)	aa	Land of Multimillion Dollar Views (multiple locations)

Big Blessing Medical Center
1 God's Reward Lane
Under the sun, State
555-555-1111

Interrogatory number five requested current employment specifics including current salary, bonuses, incentives, and non-monetary benefits which I provided. Other interrogatories requested specifics about my intention to seek equitable relief, attorney's fees, compensatory damages for emotional pain, suffering, inconvenience, mental anguish, loss of enjoyment of life and other nonpecuniary losses or future losses. I addressed financial loss due to forced early retirement, loss of yearly bonus, loss of salary, and attorney fees.

I did not request other compensation other than FMLA sick leave reimbursement. In eighteen years, three months, and fifteen days of employment, I have not had to use sick leave or annual leave under the Federal Medical Leave Act. Because of the hostile work environment created by Mr. Director and Dr. Chief of Staff at leadership meetings in front of peers, morning reports in front of peers, publicly in the river newspapers, media news report and in other public venues, threat of suspension of medical privileges, threat of reprimand, and more, I was unable to work under conditions which became intolerable. Additionally, my privileges were suspended without cause and I was served a reprimand proposal without cause. My job, my medical license, my career, and my livelihood were in jeopardy, creating intense anxiety and insomnia.

Because my privileges were summarily suspended, I could not start my new position at the East Coast Medical Center, a loss of a job promotion and opportunity to continue my career at the organization. I was unable to secure another job within the organization because of the professional slander by the facility.

Because I could not work at FBTRHCS due to the harassment and humiliation and due to the inability to secure another facility position, I was forced to retire early resulting in a retirement penalty of over a thousand dollars per month, just shy of a full twenty years. If I could have secured another position within the organization, I would have been able to continue on as an employee.

Mr. Director summarily suspended my privileges twice in the spring of 2017. Following internal and external medical chart reviews, the director had no choice but to fully reinstate my privileges at the end of Spring 2017.

In the summer of 2017, the chief of staff served me a proposal for reprimand charging that I failed to follow policy regarding opioid safety, very similar to the reason for summarily suspending my privileges. I had seven days to respond to Dr. Chief of Staff. Mr. Human Resource Chief required a face-to-face meeting to discuss the reprimand proposal with Dr. Chief of staff one week later and he set the meeting date in stone. I previously scheduled an interview with a medical center out west at that time which meant I had to inconveniently change my travel plans. Dr. Chief of Staff then chose to take leave and he failed to attend the meeting. In the absence of Dr. Chief of staff, I met with Dr. Deputy Chief of Staff (DCOS). Dr. DCOS contacted me at home while I was injured asking me to return to my associate chief of staff (ACOS) for primary care position because I was so good at my job. The reprimand was not approved in the end; but because I was interviewing for a new job, I had to disclose this possibility because I had to wait for the decision.

Also, prior to this time, I lost my position as Medical Director, East Coast Medical Center, a promotion which I accepted during the site visit in the spring of 2017. I put an offer on a house and it was accepted. My privileges were suspended three days later and I was to start my new job in a month. Dr. COS at East Coast Medical Center waited for resolution initially; but later he expressed he could not wait for the resolution of my privileges, and the facility selected their second-choice candidate.

I interviewed for two other promotional opportunities, Chief of Staff at Too Close to the River State Medical Center and Primary Care Service Line Director at History State Medical Center. References were checked and I received promising feedback and glowing reviews. I believe that in the end, the political press that followed me ("Google" my name) made these facilities nervous and I was not hired. I did disclose the situation I was in initially and why I was leaving my present position. The facilities requested references immediately after the interviews and I received good feedback.

I had two significant physical injuries requiring extensive rehabilitation in the summer of 2017 and I was out for rehabilitation and Family Medical Leave Act (FMLA) for extreme situational anxiety and insomnia resulting from the harassment. This harassment and constant threat of termination, loss of privileges, and reprimand proposals prevented my return to the Facility by the River Health Care System under the leadership of Mr. Director and Dr. Chief of Staff at this point. It became obvious that these two executive leaders, politely stated, were not supportive and looked for ways to terminate or punish me after more than fifteen years of service at the large health care system and just short of a full twenty-year retirement from the organization.

I since learned that the Ignorant Oversight Body (IOB) released a report in the spring of 2017 which was very flawed. I testified to this fact recently to the IOB just prior to my unplanned early retirement in the fall of 2017. Ms. Politician reviewed the IOB report and wrote a letter to the director of the organization which included demands. Additionally, the news story extremely embarrassed and intensely angered Mr. Director. Instead of supporting our opioid safety initiative efforts, Mr. Director and Dr. Chief of Staff chose to use me as the facility's "scapegoat" as a knee-jerk reaction directly due to anger and secondarily to appease Ms. Politician. Mr. Director's and Dr. Chief of Staff's actions were under investigation with an ERO investigation and the ERO cited significant harassment on the part of Mr. Director's and Dr. Chief of Staff's actions and other investigating bodies became involved in the activities of FBTRHCS. Dr. Chief of Staff stated to me that the IOB report was flawed and he intended to call the board members to inform them. This was on or about the spring of 2017. He announced this to the Professional Standards Board at that time also.

I did not see the Ignorant Oversite Body (IOB) report until it was included in my reprimand proposal in the summer of 2017. Dr. Chief of Staff's testimony to the Accountability Office of the IOB from the spring of 2017 was included in the reprimand binder delivered to my home under certified receipt mail in the summer of 2017. His testimony is filled with untruths (lies) regarding a history of disciplining me for opioid safety, reason for Ms. Nurse Practitioner no longer being a facility employee, and performance by Dr. PCP in the clinic.

I actually received an outstanding proficiency in fiscal year 2016 citing leadership ability and OSI efforts/accomplishments and fully satisfactory (highest rating) on my midterm proficiency just two weeks prior to the summary suspension of my privileges in the spring of 2017. I was not disciplined; I was praised. The Accountability Office of the IOB investigators asked for proof. Dr. Chief of Staff could not provide disciplinary evidence because he no evidence existed. The disciplinary incident presented by Dr. Chief of Staff was fictitious.

Fully educated and aware, Dr. Chief of Staff actively participated, and fully supported our OSI efforts. He received praise by regional leaders about our improvement. Mr. Director received praise too for all of our efforts. Weekly, our service line presented and submitted reports with data. Monthly, detailed reports prepared by Mr. AO Primary Care, were sent to the regional office. From the regional office, regional opioid safety initiative reports were reviewed with the executive leadership team monthly. It should have been clear to all that we shined. Somehow, all of these efforts were forgotten, conveniently.

I was personally and professional humiliated in front of a group of seventy-five to one hundred peers and Mr. Director stood by and smiled as the host of the leadership event. As opioid safety initiative facility champion, I lost the ability as a leader to apply opioid safety initiatives at the primary care level for our facility. A non-medical, nonclinical leader, Mr. Director, made it clear he and other leaders did not respect me as a leader. Essentially, I could not carry out my medical, ethical, legal, and professional duties as ACOS for primary care and opioid safety champion when my privileges were suspended. Not only was I affected, the other leaders were also affected, fearing the same treatment by Mr. Director and they expressed their concerns as a group.

Mr. Director targeted other employees as "scapegoats" in response to the political environment including but not limited to Dr. PCP at the main facility, Dr. PCP, Ms. RN Nurse Manager at another community clinic, Dr. PCP, Ms. PCP, NP at the community clinic, Mr. Chief of Engineering, and Dr. Chief of Surgery. Not only did I personally suffer, others suffered when I became ineffective as a service line director, opioid safety champion, and colleague.

The next interrogatories requested information about witnesses to be called, depositions to be requested, expert testimony, documents to be included, facts, opinions, hearsay of the case, documents, compensatory agreements, and reimbursements. We objected to this broad request. The list I prepared proved to be too long and onarous.

The notebooks I kept throughout my career proved helpful in responding to the next interrogatory requesting notes, diaries, memoranda, and other written documents. I copied and sent a couple hundred pages of my hand written notes from my notebooks. I laughed when my attorney mentioned this would drive them crazy. I laughed out loud again. I can't even read my own writing sometimes. My handwritting fits the stereotypic handwriting of a doctor.

We objected to interrogatories requesting bylaws, handbooks, directives, memoranda, letters, pamphlets, regulations, federal statutes, rules relating to the case and actions alleged against me. Again, the list I provided to my attorney was too long and the request too broad. We referred to previously submitted responses to additional requests for contact names and numbers, previously filed complaints with case numbers, and other redundant requests.

In response to the interrogatory regarding the East Coast Medical Center opportunity and how my whistleblowing activity caused another person to be hired, I replied:

I filled out applications for leadership positions on the company website. Within a few days, I interviewed for the Chief of Staff position at Too Close to the River State Facility by clinical video. I interviewed well and they asked me for references. References were called the next day and I knew I was leaving Facility by the River Health Care System. I was cautioned about the history of the facility and opioid use there. I thought I would be of great help to them in support of applying opioid safety initiatives.

Next, the Chief of Staff from the East Coast Medical Center called me to tell me about a new leadership position they were developing on the east coast as part of their system. He thought I would be perfect for the job and he invited me for a site visit. My husband and I traveled to the east coast for the site visit. I accepted the position and we found a house. I knew I would have to turn down the Too

Close to the River State Chief of Staff position; but I hadn't heard much since all of the reference calls. The East Coast Medical Center position fit me. I would be working with the Osteopathic College, local hospitals, and politicians, networking to provide teaching opportunities and access to health care in the east.

On a weekday in the spring of 2017, the day I was traveling back from the site visit, the *Journal of the River State* published a very unflattering article. The article quoted Ms. Politician and her statements vilifying Facility by the River Health Care System and the large health care system in general. Her statements reflected one-sided deceptive reports by patients and she continuously "over advocated for patients" not understanding their clinical histories. She ultimately coerced the executive leadership team of Facility by the River Health Care System, most notably Mr. Director (possessing no clinical knowledge) and Dr. Chief of Staff to act upon inaccurate clinical reports.

On that same weekday, Media News aired a story by Ms. Idont Check Myfacts featuring three patients stating patients were "cut off (opioids) with no communication" and Ms. Politician ridiculed opioid safety efforts by the facility. The story also featured Dr. Chief of Staff for FBTRHCS, who made ill-informed comments about FBTRHCS provider practices which I found surprising since he has been supportive of our OSI efforts all along, often being recognized along with Mr. Director for our OSI best practices at FBTRHCS. I have the documentation to prove why the opioids were stopped for safety on the three interviewed patients. Ms. Politician, Ms. Idont Check Myfacts, and Dr. Chief of Staff failed to check facts prior to airing the patients' stories. These facts, of course, may not be shared publicly due to HIPAA rules which was one of the reasons I declined the interview.

My name was used extensively in a derogatory manner during the airing of the story on Media News. As previously mentioned, my photograph was released without my permission by Mr. Director violating policy and the photograph was shown throughout the story. As opioid safety provider champion for FBTRHCS and associate chief of staff for primary care with fifteen years of primary care, pain management, and opioid safety experience at the organization, I would be the physician others would turn to for advice. Chart review is a standardized practice for champions and associate chiefs of staff to use and involve reviewing the state Prescription Monitoring Program site, medication list, opioid agreement, urine drug screen, pill counts, radiographs, provider note history and other appropriate information. When the urine does not have the drug in the urine or the patient has been filling opioids in the community and at the organization regularly, the opioid agreement (reviewed and signed by the patient previously) has been violated. It is standard practice and backed by state medical law not to renew opioids at the facility if the agreement is violated. The patients are informed by a primary team member of the findings in a respectful manner. Additional care is offered.

On the day Media News report was released, my husband and I drove back to our home by the river. Dr. Chief of Staff asked me to come back early to be interviewed by an investigative body. I agreed. I planned to report back to work the next day. While driving home from the east coast, my Administrative Officer texted me a link to Media News story. Three patients were untruthful during the interview and because of Healthcare Insurance Portability and Accountability Act of 1996, I cannot elaborate further. Ms. Idont Check Myfacts, the reporter, failed to check facts. Ms. Politician, mentioned in the report, failed to check facts. Dr. Chief of Staff for Facility by the River Health Care System failed to check facts.

After hearing Media News story, I immediately sent Dr. Chief of Staff of the East Coast Medical Center the link to review. I did not want him to think I was running away from something. Dr. Chief of Staff, East Coast Medical Center, replied to me and expressed no concern stating, "This is the way the media is with the large health care system, no big deal."

Lastly, in my response regarding the interrogatory requesting me to list persons with knowledge of the OSI situation at FBTRHCS, I listed over 150 employees by name, position, and description of the knowledge each held regarding opioid safety initiative situation at FBTRHCS.

My attorney submitted interrogatory requests to the agency. He requested the facility: to list and describe all the reasons relied upon by the facility in its decision to suspecnd Dr. Sky's privileges in the spring of 2017 and provide the complete factual basis for the reasons; to list and describe all reasons relied upon by the facility in its decision to remove Dr. Sky from her position as opioid safety co-champion in the spring of 2017 and provide the complete factual basis for such reasons; list and describe all the reasons relied upon by the facility in its decision to delay reinstating Dr. Sky's privileges following the Professional Standards Board and Clinical Executive Board's recommendation that Dr. Sky's privileges be reinstated and provide the complete factual basis for such reasons; list and describe all instances in which the facility requested a legal opinion on the meaning of the state administrative code.

Documents requested included: copies of all communication between the facility employees and the news station reporters or other personnel in the year 2017; copies of all communications between FBTRHCS, headquarters, and regional employees and Mr. Director and other FBTRHCS employees regarding News Station story discussing FBTRHCS opioid policies; copies of all documents produced in relation to all investigation related to FBTRHCS opioid practices between the years 2015 and 2018, including the first Ignorent Oversight Body investigation conducted in the winter of 2016, second IOB investigation conducted in the fall of 2017, Accountability Office to the Ignorant Oversight Body investigation, regional investigations in the new year of 2018. My attorney also reguested: copies of all documents relating to action items and action plans for each responsible staff members related to an attached email exhibit; all updates and completion dates of action items and plans; copies of all documents produced in relation to and relied upon by the facility related to Dr. Sky's alleged "failure to implement opioid safety initiatives with patients in a safe and ethical manner" referenced in Dr. Sky's automatic suspension of health care privileges and restoration of health care privileges letter by Mr. Director; copies of all documents produced in the medical reviews of Dr. Sky's patient care internally and externally; copies of documents and emails by employees relating to the News Station story and Dr. Sky; copies of patient safety flags pertaining to opioids from the years 2015 to present; copies of documents related to political complaints and patient advocate tracking system records related to opioids. My attorney requested patient records by name from 2014 through the present who were involved with opioid concerns; agenda requests from headquarters, regional and local opioid safety meetings; medical staff bylaws in effect; medical director, chief of staff, and regional director criteria for evaluation and performance, eligibilty for bonuses, increase in pay or benefits; and copies of all the facility's policies and protocols regarding opioid treatment practices in effect from 2015 to the present.

Admission requests by my attorney included: admit or deny that it was Mr. Director's decision to issue Dr. Sky an automatic suspension of privileges; admit or deny that FBTRHCS Professional Standards Board did not recommend Dr. Sky be issued an automatic suspension of privileges; admit or deny the recommendations to issue the automatic suspension of privileges was made by FBTRHCS PSB chairman Dr. Chief of Staff; admit or deny the PSB unanimously recommended that Dr. Sky's suspension of privileges be lifted and her responsibility as associate chief of staff of primary care be restored.

Lastly, my attorney submitted a notice of intent to depose Dr. Chief of Staff, Dr. Deputy Chief of Staff, Mr. Director, Ms. Secretary to the Director with the right to amend or supplement the list as needed.

CHAPTER 5
Patience My Dear Child, All in God's Timing

It's not how much faith you have, but who your faith is in.

Faith is more of a decision than a feeling. Jesus' shoulders are big enough for your stresses.

—Jason Stonehouse

It was Christmas Eve and David and I were driving back from a wonderful trip to Salt Lake City, Utah and a visit with David's brother, Don and his family. We shopped at Park City, enjoyed a western lunch, visited our favorite gallery, and reminisced about other family gatherings. The next day we snuck in more shopping at the most highly decorated Christmas area in the city and made off like bandits with 70 percent off savings for name brand goods. At the last moment we zoomed up to Sundance. Just being there warmed our hearts. The ski slopes gleamed above us. Warming fire pits lit the sky. The fires were strategically placed on the grounds in order for visitors to stroll down the walkways, view the rustic buildings glowing with white lights and greenery, and warm admirers in the embers of the fire. I enjoyed asking other families if I could take their photographs so they could all be in the photo. They welcomed the opportunity to capture their special memories together as a family and I received praise about how I marked their visit in time. Our family ended up in a quaint little area of the resort and watched a talented duo showcase their God-given talents on the guitar and fiddle. Meanwhile, a fire casted a glow from the adjoining room and the ambiance enveloped us.

David's nephew trained as an intern at Sundance I learned. He shared his experiences working with Robert Redford as a crew member intern, mostly polishing his sound skills at that time. His real surprise came with the unexpected meeting of Sally Field. He now works in Los Angeles as part of the film industry, supplementing his income parking cars. You may think parking cars sounds boring; but our nephew parks cars for stars at red carpet events such as the Golden Globe and Academy Award events. Not too shabby. We are proud of our nephew's accomplishments.

As we drove home to big sky country, my mind wandered back to my case. Our legal hearing took place in the summer of 2018 and the outcome was still pending. The judge announced at the end of the trial that he would rule within three months. When three months came, he put in some time type of legal stay for another month. Both deadlines came and went. What is up with our system?

David and I do not expect our case to ever be settled. Whistleblowing cases, no matter where they occur, take years to settle, if they settle. We know the large organization sits on a boat load of money and stalls at all levels as a mode of operation. If the judge rules in our favor, and he should rule in our favor hands down (we had all the evidence and the large health care system had little to none), the next step we expect the large health care organization to take is to appeal. As I previously described and will review now, the appeals board only has one of three members and the only member is soon retiring. There will no longer be any appeals board because of political red tape. Right now, a room is filled with appeals cases and the one remaining board member pulls out a case daily, makes his recommendations and then goes onto the next. Because the other members have not been politically appointed, the final decisions cannot be made. When this final member retires soon, all his work will be in vain. If a board ever gets appointed, and this will take years to occur, the new members will start all over, most likely ignoring the work already done if they are of a different party. *Politian* is a bad word I wrote in my last book. So is *politics*.

David and I crave a ruling however. We wonder what God's plan is in all of this for our good and His glory. This excites us. There must be a reason why we wait so long. Another lesson on patience? We believe it is more than a lesson on patience or forbearance.

Meanwhile, just last week I heard from my good friend who fought a different political battle, but her battle addressed the same large health care system. I worked with her in the land of cornfields and soybeans. At the time, I sat on a professional board to review charges against her quality of care alleged by her overzealous boss, who I admired. However, I questioned the boss's ability to keep her obsessiveness reigned in when it came to her leadership abilities. At that time, the board ruled in favor of this provider who was a colleague of mine at the time. Since leaving the land of corn and soybeans, I learned of her subsequent plight while I was suffering through mine.

In the spring of 2018, my new good friend reached out to speak with me. I learned of her incredible battle with the large health care system and my mind reeled. The same obsessive leader joined forces with other less than admirable leaders and colluded a scheme with the chief of staff, director, and board members. The facility fired Jordan. I knew all of these people except for the director. I knew what Jordan faced. I left that facility because I saw through their motives at that time which were self-serving and the leadership group's behavior was just plain mean. I listened. I empathized. I grew angry on her behalf. I shared my story with Jordan and provided the name of my outstanding attorney. Secondly, I spoke to Jordan about another one of my friends whose duty station involves sitting in a remote room at the river city facility, twiddling his thumbs for over a year at the time as another whistle blowing victim of the large health-care system. I encouraged Jordan to call Paul. Paul would be an encouragement. Lastly, I rejoiced with Jordan about how God brought me out of the tribulation to an amazing job in big sky country. I could tell this encouraged her as she sincerely expressed how happy she was for me and how good I sounded. Jordan asked me to pass her number onto Paul. They continue to share their struggles and challenges, each one of them encouraging the other. Brothers and sisters in Christ share a special bond and we are all children of God.

I received texts regularly from Jordan and we found time to connect by telephone. Whenever I saw her number pop up, I answered immediately. She prayed for ministering warring angels to bombard every step of my path, the paperwork, the courts, and everybody who touches the case. She said she was proud of me (so touching). Most of all, she thanked me for believing in her and I did!

I reminded Jordan that we have truth and God on our side. I shared photographs of our new home in the mountains, mule deer in our yard, and awesome sunsets over the mountains. She replied that when she becomes discouraged, she thinks of me living in big sky country working at a job I love even better (no comparison actually). These thoughts inspire her. She says, "God has us covered!" He sure does!

Someone at Jordan's facility shared with her that things were getting "nasty" and she was to blame. I encouraged her to let the ugly rumors "roll off her shoulders" and I shared my attorney's statement, "The more they do to you, the more ammo we have…"; but I recognized rumors are difficult to squash and to endure. I proceeded to write a letter on Jordan's behalf for her case. I knew how nasty political ladder-climbers could be and I knew her leaders all too well. Jordan hired an encouraging attorney that she trusts also. He tells her to be "strong and courageous." When she replies with discouragement, he says "be stronger and more courageous!" Amen.

Jordan exhausted all of her resources to settle the claims against her. Gossip proved to be the heart of the lies. Her attorney continued to move her forward stating, "I don't care what their decision is, we will fight this to the end and we will win!" She then proceeded to motivate me stating, "So will you!" Several days later, the facility fired Jordan.

As my husband and I traveled to the river city by automobile for the Legal Battle Board hearing in June 2018, I took photographs along the way and shared them with Jordan. I kept her updated on my case. We prayed for one another. We quoted scriptures of encouragement and strength, rejection of spiritual doubt, and thanked God in advance.

Our legal days in court came and went. We should win, hands down, without any doubt whatsoever in a fair world. The verdict is still out. We continue to put our faith in God and His plans.

David and I returned home following a brief visit with our family in the Great Lakes after my days in court. Exhausted, I rested and remained fairly quiet during the visit. Our family supported us. As summer bloomed, we enjoyed God's country, often four wheeling right outside of our back door. We rode for miles and miles on unending trails, often spotting wildlife including moose, bear, deer, and elk. We discovered hidden waterfalls which gushed from melting snow-topped mountains above. We found hidden lakes surrounded by towering evergreens and aspens. Best of all, we were alone in the mountains most of the time. Who gets to experience God's masterpieces alone? This hidden gem strengthened our belief that God set us on the rock in a setting above and beyond anything we could have imagined ourselves. God blessed our faithfulness. We gave Him all the praise and glory. Selah.

I shared the photos from big sky country with Jordan and invited her out for a visit. She planned to visit soon and she did! I texted her encouraging songs such as *Stronger* by Mandesa, *Fear is a Liar* by Zach Williams, *What He Said* by Group 1 Crew stating these are theme songs I held onto and played frequently.

Jordan's hearing was scheduled for the fall of 2018. I shared the faith chapter of Hebrews 11 with her. She and her attorney ended up conferring with my attorney. It was helpful. I started a prayer warrior group by text to expand the amount of prayers going up to God. There were twenty of us on the list. I texted, "Dear Brothers and Sisters in Christ, Jordan, who is on this group, will need our prayers starting early tomorrow for three days as she battles the large health-care system at her hearing. You all were such warriors for me and I hope we can all encourage and pray for Jordan. May the LORD reveal the truth during the hearing and GOD be glorified. This is my prayer. Thank you for being supportive of me. Let us raise Jordan up in prayer. "God has you in his hands Jordan!!!"

My friends began sending prayers by text for us all to see as encouragement with emojis such as prayer hands and crosses.

Introverts chimed in with "AMENs." Prayer warriors prayed for truth in the case, comfort, peace and confidence for Jordan as she testifies. Some prayed for wisdom and boldness as she goes against the giant. Requests for grace and mercy were lifted up in Jesus's name. Jordan expressed her gratitude for the prayer warriors. My pastor sent a prayer with scripture:

"For whatever is born of God overcomes the world. And this is the victory that has overcome the world-our world." (1 John 5:4, NKJV)

He lifted Jordan up in prayer asking for love, grace, mercy, truth and victory. He asked for the father's presence during the days to come in the name of Jesus. Another amen.

Jordan shared a brief biography with the group which moved us all. More people responded sincerely with prayers and acknowledged they were praying. And they were! One of my friends adamantly encouraged us all to keep the prayers going. And they did! One sister sent devotional scriptures, another acknowledged our awesome God that we can call on 24-7, another reminded us of God's awesome power, another sent a thumbs up emoji and there was plenty of scripture. Prayer warriors prayed. AMENs abounded. Praises and glory to God echoed.

The prayer warriors texted messages of encouragement throughout Jordan's day with the board. Everyone of us felt useful and blessed to be part of such a supportive group. It humbled us to pray together and express our actions through text messaging. Following the closing of the board meeting, friends each wrote that in some way, they felt honored to be asked for their support and they were part of something bigger. They felt part of this life's journey and calling to serve a mighty and awesome God. We felt the Holy Spirit in our presence. We loved our neighbor as ourselves, God's second greatest commandment.

Fall of 2018 turned into winter and just before Christmas, I received the most exciting call from Jordan. She won her case. She won her case! Hallelujah! Praise the Lord! Glory and honor to God Almighty!

I wrote this to the prayer warriors, "I am praising the LORD for some amazing glorious news!!!! Jordan won!!! She has been fully restored in her position. Plus, she has a great financial victory which is an amazing blessing for her. Thank you all for your prayers. GOD is sooooooo good. All the time!!! I am proud of you Jordan! FYI the private sector is great…in big sky country anyway."

Jordan responded, "Your prayers went straight from your lips to God's ears. I am thanking God for all of you and wishing you great blessings and peace in a meaningful life ahead in 2019."

My pastor replied, "To God be the Glory. But thanks be to God, who gives us the victory through our Lord Jesus Christ. Therefore, my beloved brethren, be steadfast, immovable, always abounding in the work of the Lord, knowing that your labor is not in vain in the Lord." (1 Corinthians 15:57–58, NKJV)

Our friends reminded us about Jesus carrying us in "Footprints." We are building that bridge of faith. God is surely orchestrating our paths. We stood in awe of Jesus.

As of Christmas 2018, I still waited for the outcome of the Legal Battle Board hearing. Six months had passed. I still waited. The anchor holds. My faith is sound. God's timing is different than ours and His is best. I wait.

CHAPTER 6

The Friend God Called Me to Visit on My Last Day before Retirement

> God is big enough for your challenges. God is not intimidated by our fears, struggles or difficulties. Jesus overcame sin and death when He was resurrected to make a way for us to live differently. Trust Him and rest in His strength.
>
> —Jason Stonehouse

I remember my last days at the Facility by the River Health Care System fondly. My department celebrated my accomplishments and showed their support by having a pot luck luncheon. I enjoyed the company and felt appreciated. We talked about my future plans and I encouraged my colleagues to press on, knowing they served a special community who needed them to stay strong. As we were sharing, one of my administrative officers unexpectedly stood up and commanded our attention. What he spoke next, I cannot remember with accuracy; but I knew I earned the respect of someone I respected and admired greatly. One by one, others spoke boosting my shattered confidence, validating my efforts I believed were all in vain at the time. I felt loved. I could move on without regret.

While at a different location of our facility to check out of the Facility by the River Health Care System, I felt this need to try to find a friend of mine that I recently heard was removed from his leadership position in engineering. I could not believe it was true. Convinced I could not leave without making a sincere effort to locate my colleague, I set out on a mission. I found him in a remote location on campus in a dilapidated building. I knocked on the door. I heard deadbolts twisting and the door unlocked noisily. There stood Paul.

I must have looked shocked; but shock passed to happiness to find Paul, especially in that particular location. I worked with Paul at our main campus in the engineering office two years prior to this meeting. I informed him that this day was my last day working for the large health-care system. He asked me to step outside, out of the building. We shared our stories. Both of our jaws dropped as each one of us expounded on our circumstances put forth into motion by our prestigious executive leader team members. I thought my situation landed high on the list of legal infractions; but Paul's predicament topped mine ten-fold.

We encouraged one another as colleagues, comrades, and as a brother and sister in Christ. We believed God had an amazing plan for His glory and our good. This gave us peace. He quoted the prophecy of Luke 12:3: "Therefore, whatsoever ye have spoken in darkness shall be heard in the light; and that which ye have spoken in the ear in closets shall be proclaimed upon the housetops." This visit ignited a long friendship and a support system that would soon include many others needing our support and guidance. To God be the glory.

CHAPTER 7
The First Data Dump by the Agency

> May the God of hope fill you with all joy and
> peace as you trust in Him, so that you may over-
> flow with hope by the power of the Holy Spirit.
> —Romans 15:13 (NIV)

In the spring of 2018, I received almost three thousand pages of responses from the agency. One of the first reports I received came from an internal quality clinical review of patient medical charts from the Facility by the River Health Care System. In summary, sixty-six random charts were reviewed; but not all of the charts fit questions involved in the review so the numbers vary.

Fifty-seven out of sixty-four charts contained valid pain agreements (89% compliant). Of the seven consents which were past due when the order was placed, all were updated within ten days to three months when the patients presented for scheduled appointments or when the provider returned from leave. The reviewer documented that I recognized expired contracts, reviewed the prescription data base, checked urine drug screens, and made clinical decisions to renew the medication and arranged follow up with the patients' providers. It was noted that I alerted the primary care providers. One chart mentioned involved a taper off of the medication which was already in progress so a contract would no longer be needed. All of the expired pain agreements were recognized by the clinical staff and addressed.

The reviewer described the Prescription Management Program (PMP) in detail and stated I was in 97 percent compliance. Of the two searches not documented, I ordered a one-month supply of medication and requested a new urine drug screen which came back abnormal. The patient was informed of the finding and that the medication would no longer be filled. The reviewer stated that I checked the state PMP on the other patient who fell out, but the check was one month overdue. In reality, the state PMP was checked and documented, but it fell out due to the criteria given to the reviewer to follow.

I complied with checking urine drug screens on sixty-one out of sixty-five charts (94 percent compliance rate). Of the four charts which fell out, I requested completion of the urine drug screens. Lastly, all of the patients requiring tapering of their opioids were completed appropriately 100 percent of the time.

Included in the data dump material was the Ignorant Oversight Body's (IOB) report from the winter of 2017. It contained the inaccurate report by the committee perpetuating the assumption that my actions pertaining to opioid safety were unsafe. Prior to the date of this report, I had been clinically redeemed by a clinical investigator citing my tapers were 100 percent safe. Other aspects of my clinical care related to opioid safety were deemed appropriate and necessary as well. To my dismay, The Ignorant Oversight Body ignored the clinical investigator's highly relevant facts. The IOB conveniently ignored the clinical report. The whirlwind that followed escalated and perpetuated the inaccurate IOB report. The only good thing that resulted was that Dr. Chief of Staff was put in the hot seat this time. Dr. Chief of Staff failed to address the inaccuracy of the IOB report as he planned, intentionally or unintentionally. Little did he know, his failure to act would soon come back to bite him in the keister.

Mr. Director, a retired army leader, concerned himself with his image first and data second. He focused on patient satisfaction scores. Unfortunately, our facility was at the bottom of this survey. This was no surprise to most of us since the facility chose to focus on opioid safety initiatives during this timeframe. Other facilities previously addressed opioid safety and previously sailed that ship of low patient satisfaction scores which goes along with making opioid safety changes. I survived that rough road previously while at the facility in the land of cornfields and soybeans along with the facility by the great lakes. We endured the poor ratings, choosing to save lives knowing we would recover. We chose safety over satisfaction. This choice was the right thing to do clinically.

Mr. Director blamed my opioid safety efforts regarding our facility landing in the lowest 20 percent rung in patient satisfaction ratings. I accepted the heat he blew my way in the name of saving lives. Dr. Chief of Staff would remind Mr. Director that my efforts and success in increasing employee satisfaction on the employee survey and success in hiring was reflected in the *quality* section of the full report. Mr. Director did not care. He wanted it all and he wanted me gone.

In the fall of 2017, the Ignorant Oversite Board (IOB) paid another visit to the Facility by the River Health Care System (FBTRHCS). Mr. Director testified under oath and shared his dismay about all of the "hot calls" by highly visible company entities. He told the investigators he was told to "stay on top of them (the highly visible political cases)."

The IOB began building upon their inaccurate report with a new premise. They wanted blood from Dr. Chief of Staff this time in order to satisfy a particular politician, Ms. Politician from the river state. Remember, the IOB received a report that the medical records of the patients from the community clinic in the river state had all been reviewed and I, Dr. Sky, tapered correctly and safely 100 percent of the time. The IOB chose to ignore this significant finding. They chose to avoid embarrassment by deciding not to publicly state they errored in their report. The IOB chose to perpetuate their inaccurate report and build upon it. As my husband reminds me, that is what happens when the organization provides oversight to the organization. What do you expect?

I expected integrity, commitment, advocacy, respect, and excellence; the values of organization ingrained in us as employees. Mr. Director, Dr. Chief of Staff, and the other executive leaders of the organization wore the company value logo on their jackets; but none of them incorporated these values into their hearts.

CHAPTER 8

The Fuel of Encouragement

God is able to make all grace abound to you,
so that having all sufficiency in all things at all
times, you may abound in every good work.
— 2 Corinthians 9:8 (ESV)

I often felt alone in my misery. I avoided contact with others at the Facility by the River Health Care System. I realized others did not know what to say to me. Some asked me if I was back in action yet. Others went about their duties as if nothing happened. I knew my coworkers feared retaliation if they supported me. Some colleagues supported me despite this fear. For them I will be forever grateful.

I received the following electronic email correspondences from a service line leader colleague:

> I am embarrassed and appalled at the "way" this went "down." You have my 100% support. Thank you for the Herculean effort you have expended for the benefit of our patients. Not sure but I think these charts in question need to be reviewed by an outside and impartial reviewer. Not sure the best way to accomplish this. As they say... "No good deed goes unpunished."

My administrative officer kept in contact whenever he could. He wrote:

> "Just know that your efforts regardless of getting the credit helped about 3000 patients get off highly addictive (doses of) medicine and probably resulted in saving or delaying them having an accidental overdose."

At another time he texted:

> "Things that make you go hmm…slam the person that did the work and take all the credit."

Later, I received the message:

> "I'm sorry for what happened today…though I don't know all the facts of the situation, it appears that a decision has been made and as long as you feel your integrity is solid, you can walk away with head held up high…thank you for what you did and though the patients complained, I'm sure you saved a number of them from their own destructive behavior…It was an absolute honor to work for you."

I choked up after reading that message. Lastly, I read:

> "Just saw my first opioid safety flag ever placed by Dr. Chief of Staff…wonder if he had a face-to-face to discuss that."

To which I replied, "Touché!"

One colleague texted:

"In Leadership Development Day, it's not the same without you here."

And later she wrote:

"I was just talking with Chief who thought you resigned. He said he feels terrible about what's happening to you."

I received multiple contact messages from the pharmacy staff. Many of us had grown close in the opioid safety effort. Doctors did not want to write unsafe prescriptions and pharmacists did not want to fill them. We bonded. One pharmacist wrote:

"Dr. Sky: I am so sorry that you are leaving. It is a big loss for this facility. Not only to the staff but our patients. Please know the FBTR staff does support you and very much appreciates you for what you have done. People recognize there are two sides to a piece of bologna, people know you and back you. My thoughts and prayers to you and your family. I will miss working with you. Let me know if I could be helpful in the future. Best wishes.

And thanks for being you."
Tears welled in my eyes.
Often, colleagues kept me informed in support:

"I'm logged onto peer review meeting. Just discussed your case (again) about the patient who died of coronary artery disease and cardiac arrest three weeks after a methadone taper. It was UNANIMOUS to assign it a level 1 again (most practitioners would do the same). There is NO case here against you…in any venue. This should be a slam dunk for your attorney. Witch hunt as far as I'm concerned."

I texted another leader and stated I knew Mr. Director would not sign (the reinstatement of my privileges). Figures. I received an encouraging note:

> "Well, Dr. Chief of Staff needs to get his story straight because he told me that the director agreed with the PSB/CEB recommendation."

At that same time, another leader texted:

> "Dr. COS told me congratulations. I believe they all signed off because Mr. Director (finally) gave them the OK. So sorry you had to go through this. Inexcusable."

And in another conversation:

> "You are the scapegoat to get the politicians off their back. Do you intend to appeal the reprimand?"

I replied:

> "Oh, yes, I will be in tomorrow and Friday to prepare. I may even need Monday because I have so much proof."

The reply:
"You go girl. (thumbs up emoji)"

Following my untimely resignation and retirement from the organization, I heard from my primary care providers. I received heartwarming texts such as:

> "Big, I have the day off today and won't be there for your party. I just wanted to say thanks for everything you have done for all of us including the patients! I want to thank you for the extra effort you put towards making my transition into the organization as easy as possible. I wish you well and hope the best for you! Take care."

Another provider wrote:

> "Keep in touch. You are the best boss I ever had, and friend too."

Later, still another physician wrote:

> "I don't know if you are still with the organization, but just wanted to thank you for giving me this job. Miss talking to you. Take care of yourself. Call me if you need a pep talk."

One of my providers at another clinic texted:

> "Dr. Sky. Hi! I know you are busy!!! I went to Dr. PCP 4 and told him I got a text from a colleague in Richmond!!! She had seen some tv interview!!! She has heard me sing your praises and really knows how much I respect you (prayer hands emojis). I have told her over and over when I started this job that the only reason I stay is because I have an advocate who believes that we have to do the right thing!!! I told her that I was very shocked to see the respect and support

for the clinical providers, especially (from) the ACOS!!!"

She later contacted me and texted:

"Dr. Sky, Enjoy the beautiful west, it is truly God's country!!! BTW, I AM GOING TO LEAVE THIS CIRCUS!!! Without you it is impossible to navigate!!! God Bless!!!!! I will give you an update."

Later:

"I will stand with you on any level. You have been a role model in honesty, integrity, and leadership that is not a common finding in this setting!!!I would've left week one had it not been for you!!! I don't know what or how to help show the disasters you have averted."

I am smiling as I recall messages such as:

"Just wanted to say hi! Thought about you as I'm studying for the boards too. Hope everything is going well for you. Will catch up after the boards. Miss you n luv you too."

How many bosses are loved by their employees? I must have done something right.

The primary care providers continued to contact me.

"Hi Dr. Sky, glad to know you are happy and settling down. You are missed here too." "Hope you are doing well. We wish you the best. We support you for all you have done.
HAPPY NEW YEAR. BEST WISHES."

I receive telephone calls too. Every now and then, one of the docs will give me a call asking about my case. Great rumors such as I won and received a million dollars makes me laugh. I wonder where rumors start. I liked that one! I wish it were true. I replied to keep that one going. It would be good for the bad guys to get a hold of that one...

CHAPTER 9

My Attorney's Response to the First Data Dump

Let us hold unswervingly to the hope we profess,
for He who promised is faithful. And let us consider how we may spur one another on toward
love and good deeds.
—Hebrews 10:23–24 (NIV)

The first data dump, 2,868 pages of information the agency submitted for my case, contained some valuable documents including the
stellar internal quality review of my opioid safety cases, supportive
Administrative Board report, flawed Ignorant Oversight Body report,
perjured testimony by Dr. Chief of Staff to the IOB, self-serving letters by Ms. Politician to headquarters with her uneducated demands,
shocking provider turnover statistics, perjured testimony by Dr.
Deputy Chief of Staff, Dr. Medicine's glowing testimony, my IOB
testimony, Ms. PCP Nurse Practitioner's revealing testimony to the
IOB, other physicians' treasured testimonies to the IOB, invaluable
nursing testimonies to the IOB, honest pharmacist testimonies to the
IOB, and many other helpful and not-so-helpful reports. As I read
through each page of the data dump, I became aware of the super-
abundant events that transpired without my knowledge. With these
documents in hand, I gained an uncanny awareness of my situation.
Many of the testimonies vindicated my case as clinical staff reported
to the investigative bodies. Political and executive leaders' testimonies pointed fingers in my direction, despising me, blaming me as

the cause to their current plights. Their current plights followed as consequences to actions taken in response to their own selfish and aggressive desires to climb the ladder of success and to where? In my opinion, uninformed politicians and ambitious leaders blindly seek public approval, ignore truth, and subsequently harm others who unintentionally get in their way.

My attorney replied to the agency's interrogatory and document requests as follows:

Interrogatories 1, 2, and 3

The interrogatories call for a description of the "complete factual basis" which is a defined term in the interrogatory definition section. When a discovery request asks for the "COMPLETE FACTUAL BASIS" for any contention, statement, defense, claim, allegation, belief or conclusion, the response shall include, but not be limited to, the description, identification and enumeration of: (1) all facts relating in any way to the contention, statement, defense, claim, allegation, belief or conclusion; (2) each and every document that records, reflects or relates in any way to such facts; (3) each and every statement or item of testimonial or other evidence that relates in any way to such facts; and (4) the name of each and every person consulted, relied on, or with knowledge for the substantiation of such contention, statement, defense, claim, allegation, belief or conclusion.

In particular (but without limitation), please DESCRIBE the "close examination of the Facility by the River policy and the state law cited in the policy" referred to in the Agency's referred to in the Agency's response to Appellant's Interrogatory 3 including all issues which the Agency needed to resolve during the delay, who Dr. Chief of Staff and Mr. Director consulted with to resolve those issues, and what information Dr. Chief of Staff and Mr. Director learned that resolved such issues.

Interrogatory 4

Attorney client privilege is waived when a party invokes reliance on legal advice as part of their defense. The Agency, in its jurisdictional brief, asserted that one of its key defenses in the case is reliance on a very questionable interpretation of State Administrative Code 844 5-6-6, thus waiving privilege. The Agency waived privilege a second time in its response to Interrogatory 3, where Dr. Chief of Staff asserted that "the only delay was due to close examination of the Facility by the River policy and the state law cited in the policy." Those two defenses placed the interpretation of State Administrative Code 844 5-6-6 directly at issue, thus waiving all privilege relating to communications regarding interpretation of State Administrative Code 844 5-6-6.

Therefore, please respond to this interrogatory.

Document Requests 1 and 2

I am skeptical that these are all the responsive documents in the Agency's possession. Please provide the search terms and methods used to find these documents and verify that they are the only responsive documents in the Agency's possession.

Document Requests 3 and 14

These document requests encompass the current/recent investigation instigated at the direction of the region regarding the medical center's response to Dr. Sky's opioid practices and the medical center's opioid practices generally. The Agency's response did not include any documents related to that investigation (including transcripts, meeting minutes, emails, etc.) or any objection to providing such documents. Please provide them.

Document Requests 5 and 6

The Agency's response did not include any external reviews of Dr. Sky's patient care as requested in both these Document Requests. Neither has the Agency objected to providing such reviews. Please provide them.

Document Request 8

The Agency has simply provided a raw list redacted in such a way as to provide no information whatsoever. In addition, it has failed to provide "all flag information for flagged patients" or "any additional comments or patient information contained therein." The Patient Drug Seeking Flag and Opioid Safety Flag list is linked to comments that are used by providers in understanding why the flags were put in place. Please provide such information and do so in a way that the redacted information can be linked to the other responsive information (for example, the documents requested in Requests 9 and 10).

Document Request 9

This does not appear to be a complete list of responsive records. As discussed in the comments to Document Requests 10 and 11 below, please do a search for "Flagged Patients" (a defined term in the discovery request) and in addition, the spreadsheet provided by the agency cuts off much of the text contained in the records, please provide a complete version. Further, please provide a method by which the parties can link the redacted records to other records for the same patients. Please note that these documents are highly responsive and in many cases name Dr. Sky personally.

Document Request 10

The Agency has failed to respond to this request. The cited records are simply a list of the interrogatories and a single email from Ms. AO to the Chief of Staff saying she doesn't know how to do a search. However, "flagged" patients are a specific universe of patients (which should be well known to many employees of the Agency) as discussed above and below, and it would be simple for the Agency to pull that flagged list, search those names in the politician complaints tracking system, and then redact the results (in a way that can be matched to other patient records). Please do so.

Document Request 11

"Flagged patients" is a term of art within the medical center and refers to about 350 specific patients whose have exhibited behavior or other factors that warrants caution in further prescription of opioids to those patients. They are easily searchable in the Agency's databases (the purpose of the flag is to make them easily searchable) and supplying this information would be simple for the Agency. Further, the information is directly relevant to the case because Dr. Sky's disclosures were specifically regarding the Agency's handling of those flagged patients. In addition and in the alternative, the Agency's objections to not reply to providing records for the specifically named patients, which the Agency could have done easily at any time since the discovery request was served, even if it was not aware of how its flag system worked and the limited number of patients who are so flagged in the system is not acceptable. Finally, 38 U.S.C. § 7332 specifically contemplates release of information under a court order and is not a reason to object to discovery. In addition, the parties discussed redacting the information under pseudonyms or other redactions, and the Agency can do so in this case. The QM system prints out the flagged list in a spreadsheet, and the Agency can simply redact the names section (with acronyms). Therefore, please provide the information requested.

Document Request 13

Please provide Opioid Safety Initiative Workgroup agendas and minutes (the Agency only provided documents for the Pain Management Committee, which is a separate body with separate minutes and agendas). In the past, these were kept in the possession of Mr. COS Secretary.

CHAPTER 10

Recredentialing Scare

> May the LORD bless you and protect you. May
> the LORD smile on you and be gracious to you.
> May the LORD show you HIS favor and give
> you His peace.
> —Numbers 6:24–26 (NLT)

Every two years, physicians needed to reapply for hospital and clinical privileges at the Facility by the River Health Care System and large health care system overall. My expiration date for practicing medicine landed right in the middle of the retaliatory efforts by the chief of staff and director. My heart sank…again.

The credentialing officer sent the following letter:

Subject: Reappointment time
Dr. Sky,

It is time to start the reappointment process for your appointment is currently terms Fall of 2016.

I have re-opened your file so you can make your updated entries to complete the reappointment process.

I attached a cover letter which has your log in information and what is needed to complete the process.

I have a packet of credentialing materials which I will drop off at your office.

Please contact me if you have any questions about the process. Thank you,

Credentialing Specialist
FBTRHCS

I replied:

Sent: Summer 2017
To: Mr. Credentialing (BTRHCS)
Subject: [EXTERNAL] Re: Dr. B. Sky

Hi Mr. Credentialing,

I completed the credentialing package. Do you send reference forms out to Dr. ACOS, Dr. PCP3, and Dr. PCP9 or do I?

Thank you for your assistance and for keeping me informed. I will be picking up my packet on Sunday at the office. I hope to return soon so that my FMLA will not be as much of a factor in re-credentialing. Please hold off as long as possible and/or keep me informed as to when I will be scheduled for PSB if you are willing. I have secured some assistance that will be helpful when I return.

Sincerely,
Big

Then, he responded:

Dr. Sky,

Thanks for letting me know about the credentialing file.

I will be glad to contact the references and have them return the forms directly to me.

We have some time to complete this process. I start the process a couple months ahead to avoid getting too close to appointment term dates. And I can take six to eight files to PSB at every meeting instead of one huge stack.

At this point my plan is to have your file presented to PSB Fall 2017.

Mr. Credentialing

Then, much later to my surprise:

Dr. Sky

It was good to speak with you.

Dr. Chief of Staff went ahead and signed approval to your reappointment file.

But we will need a copy of your health form for the PSB meeting. And for your file.

Technically PSB could table the file as incomplete.

Thanks

Mr. Credentialing Specialist
FBTRHCS

The fact that the chief of staff signed off on my credentialing file brought partial relief; but I knew the director had to ultimately sign the document. I believed he would not sign the document based upon previous actions. I contacted my attorney about my concerns.

Max,

I appreciated our phone conference yesterday and I am grateful to have your representation.

1. I interviewed for a private family practice job in big sky country by telephone today and spoke with Mr. CEO.

During the interview, Mr. CEO revealed to me that he Googled my name and learned of my opioid safety initiative challenges.

Not only does the unfortunate media publicity affect large health-care organization job prospects, including promotions in the organization; but the bad press affects opportunities outside of the organization as well. The damage done to my professional and personal reputation are even greater than I originally thought. It appears I will need to explain this unfortunate situation indefinitely.

Fortunately for me, I had disclosed the political concerns about the large health-care system and I asked Mr. CEO about the opioid epidemic situation in big sky country. We are on the same page in how we handle opioid safety. Good news here.

2. I am being re-credentialed at the large health-care system as part of standard re-credentialing processes (FBTRHCS Medical Bylaws). My current privileges expire in the fall of 2017. I spoke with the credentialing expert to clarify how being on FMLA affects my credentialing. I understand from Mr. Credentialing that use of FMLA would not prevent the board from granting me privileges.

   a. I believe the Professional Standards Board and Clinical Executive Board will be understanding.
   b. I am not certain that Mr. Director will sign off on the documents and ultimately, the decision is made by the director.
   c. There is some risk in staying at the organization long enough to be re-credentialed on or before the fall of 2017.

3. I may retire early and take a cut in my retirement benefits. I am considering this option seriously because if/when I return to work, I will be put right back into the position of assisting primary care providers as their supervisor with

opioid safety initiative decisions. This puts me and my credentials at great risk and is the basis of the anxiety and insomnia this situation creates for me; thus, the basis of my FMLA. I do have plenty of leave in the bank and I have some time left for consideration of my options.

a. Retiring four years early from the organization is minimally a $1,000,000.00 loss of salary and I really have no plans to stop working at age 60.
b. Retiring early from the organization results in a monthly retirement benefit loss of approximately $2000 per month, $24,000 annually for life.
c. Offers outside of the organization are $45,000.00 less annually than my current salary.

I thought this information may be helpful. Thanks again for your expertise and assistance!

Sincerely,
Big

My attorney replied:

Big, in the future, you can contact us directly.
On your questions:

1. That's really horrible. It's definitely something we will address when it comes time to write a demand letter to the agency and will factor in your damages in your case. Thank you for sending the information.
2. *"I am not certain that Mr. Director, will sign off on the documents and ultimately, the decision is made by the director."*
    Is the concern that he won't sign off on FMLA, or that he won't sign off on the re-credentialing?
    "There is some risk in staying at the organization long enough to be re-credentialed on or before the fall of 2017."

In some ways, it would work in your favor on your legal case if they don't re-credential you. There's a perverse aspect of lawsuits where the more bad things happen to you and the more blatant those things are, the better it is for your lawsuit. If they didn't re-credential you, how would the scenario play out? The boards would recommend you get re-credentialed and Mr. Director would override their decision? What basis do you think he would use to justify it and is he required to put his justification in writing?

3. What would you gain from retiring early? I understand the desire to get away from the stress of the situation, but if the worst thing they can do is try and pull your credentials (which you could appeal if necessary), wouldn't retiring early mean all of the same bad things you worried about happening to you would happen anyway through your decision to retire?

If you want, we can talk more in depth about this on the phone, I'm available late this afternoon and early next week. One thing that has helped some other clients with stress in these situations is to remember that once you start fighting the agency legally, the bad things they do to you are often <u>good</u> for you, and thinking of them that way is often stress relieving because it removes the fear that those things could happen.

Max

Much to my surprise and relief, I ended up receiving this letter:

Fall 2017
Dr. B. Sky:

This is to notify you that at the Clinical Executive Board in the fall of 2017, you were recommended for your appointment as a Licensed Independent Practitioner to the medical staff as follows:

Appointment

Department: Primary Care Services
Specialty: ACOS Primary Care / Family Medicine
Status: Staff
From/To: Primary Appointment From 2017 to 2019

A copy of your approved privileges is enclosed. Be advised there may be additional processes that HR is required to perform before your appointment is complete.

As a member of the Medical Staff, you will be expected to fulfill the following requirements:

1. Maintain your CPR certification.
2. Complete all required training modules; and
3. In the event of an emergency/disaster situation, providers with an appointment of 0.625 FTEE or greater should immediately contact their Service Chief to receive specific instructions on their assignment. Providers with an appointment less than 0.625, and all contract and WOC staff who are on duty at the organization should immediately contact their Service Chief to receive specific instructions on their assignment.

   If you remain as a FBRHCS provider, you will be asked to renew clinical privileges every two years. Please review the clinical privilege form closely for any changes to your original privilege request.

We appreciate your willingness to serve our patients and look forward to working with you. If you have any questions regarding this information, please contact me at 555-555-1234 or via email. Thank you.

Sincerely,
Mr. Credentialing
Credentialing Office

Much to my surprise and relief, the director signed off on my privileges without a fight.

CHAPTER 11
A Narcissist Will Never Settle

He will keep you strong right up to the end, and
He will keep you free from all blame on the great
day when our Lord Jesus Christ returns.
—1 Corinthians 1:8 (Daily Bible Devotional,
August 4, 2019, Coastalchurch.tv)

The judge demanded a settlement discussion and my attorney and
I eagerly agreed to submit a proposal. The director of the agency
declined a settlement offer and he failed to submit to the demands of
the judge. We submitted the following proposal:

Dr. B. Sky's Settlement Offer

Dr. Sky Proposes that the organization will:

1. Issue a finding by under Section 104 of the Dr. Chris
    Kirkpatrick Whistleblower Protection Act of 2017 (Public
    Law 115–73) that Mr. Director and Dr. Chief of Staff
    committed a prohibited personnel practice against Dr. Sky.
2. Allow Dr. Sky to submit an oral and written explanation and
    evidence on the nature and circumstances of the prohibited
    personnel practice to a headquarters official who will then
    determine what further action the Agency will take pursu-
    ant to 104(b)(1)(A)(ii) of the Kirkpatrick Act (the Deciding

Official in 104(b)(1)(A)(ii) Kirkpatrick Act determination regarding Mr. Director and Dr. Chief of Staff).

3. Issue a letter to News Station requesting that the station remove the story about Dr. Sky from its website. This letter does not need to be made public by the Agency.

4. Credit Dr. Sky with 20 years of service for the purpose of retirement benefits, or reimburse her an amount of money equivalent to that lost retirement.

5. Reimburse all attorneys' fees paid by Dr. Sky in the case.

In return Dr. Sky will:

1. Settle all claims against the Agency.

2. Agree to work in good faith with Agency personnel to improve FBTRHCS's opioid treatment procedures for a period of six months in a manner agreed upon by her and the Agency (to the extent allowed by Dr. Sky's current job responsibilities). If the amount of time spent on this goes beyond 25 hours total Dr. Sky will be paid a reasonable consulting fee in good faith for her time. Dr. Sky will not be required to work over 5 hours on any given week or for over 25 hours total without her written consent, and she will not be required to work during any time or in any way that disrupts her current job.

The director ignored the proposal. We carried on with our case, unhindered.

CHAPTER 12

Discovering the Truth through the Eyes of the Enemy; Another Data Dump

> Day by day the LORD takes care of the innocent, and they will receive an inheritance that lasts forever.
>
> —Psalm 37:18 (NLT)

Mr. Director focused on patient satisfaction even though the organization's report also included achievements regarding mortality and quality measures which is where our facility shined. The director could not accept challenges in patient satisfaction for a brief time period while we worked on opioid challenges. If he would have been willing to support the clinical staff, the story would have had a fairy tale ending. Lives would have been saved.

I learned about the conversations Mr. Director had with investigators. He acknowledged my success regarding the employee survey; but minimized the importance. He acknowledged our cohesive primary care group; but expected us to "exude our happiness onto the patients."

It soon became obvious that Mr. Director landed in the hot seat with the investigators and he did not like it. He couldn't help but speak about his displeasure about the "political call," "hot call," "other hot call," and "yet another hot call." He then had to entertain another office visit and his superior scolded him bluntly stating, "I don't want these issues to come to me. I just don't know why you guys don't fix this." "Fix this" meant get rid of me to the director, plain and simple. It was plain to see that the highly visible political inquiries infuriated Mr. Director.

The director's testimony to the investigator revealed that Mr. Director knew our facility did not have a good opioid safety policy or what was involved in following the confusing state law. In reality, nobody even knew such policy existed. He stated opioid tapering according to the state "was not 100 percent crystal clear." Mr. Director also stated the chief of staff counseled me about not following policy. The investigator replied, "If you talk to Dr. Sky, she will say that never occurred, and she has been quite vocal. She thinks she is a scapegoat for all of that…" Humm…maybe the Ignorant Oversight Body investigator did listen to my testimony after all.

The chief of staff's testimony contained a myriad of lies and nonsensical comments such as suggesting that I could have gone to the remote clinics, lined up all of the patients on opioids, visited with them face-to-face, and discussed my concerns. As I referred to in previous writing, the chief of staff and I conferenced in with a concerned primary care physician from that same location who could not see all of her patients in a month (75 slots short) let alone in an afternoon. What was he thinking? I heard him say the same thing to me at one point and laughed in his face unexpectedly because the statement was so absurd. I was in charge of two major hospitals and four rural clinics as the primary care service chief and facility opioid safety physician. Our health care system facility wrote more opioid prescriptions than most of the other facilities across the nation and had more opioid overdoses and deaths in the community than other facilities across the nation. How could one person meet with all of the patients face-to-face? At the time, many of us wondered if the chief of staff suffered from dementia. I excused his memory problems as being too busy; but as I reflect, I wonder.

Mr. HR Chief testified and clearly expressed his concerns about the chief of staff having cognitive problems. He reported his concerns to the director immediately upon the director's arrival to our facility. Mr. HR Chief and I frequently shared our observations and we both believed Dr. Chief of Staff to be a poor unsupportive leader. He spoke about the need to report certain practitioners to the National Practitioner Data Bank; but I was not one of them. He supported me. Just as I sighed with relief that I had an ally, Mr. HR Chief disappointed me. I read testimony related to a problem physician and the

HR chief stated I failed to give him evidence to support the charges. Now I wondered if *he* also had cognitive ailments. I gave Mr. HR Chief a tabbed binder filled with supporting evidence. How could he forget? At that time, the wind must have shifted and the pages in the binder took flight, never to be found. Actually, I believe the binder helped the large health care system win the lawsuit brought upon the agency by the physician due to my efforts and documentation. Her case settled quickly and she lost her case. In retrospect, I believe she may have been bullied as a strong opioid provider prior to my arrival and her subsequent challenging behavior reflected intense frustration. I tried to help her as her new boss; but the damage had been done. The chief of staff put me in the middle of a difficult situation and I am certain he failed to enlighten me to all of the facts involved. I wished the physician well. I prayed she had found peace.

Dr. Chief of Staff testified that the Professional Standards Board did not recommend a summary suspension of my privileges. This testimony contradicted a previous testimony to the same group that the PSB was not even involved. I recall my colleague stating, "Well, Mr. Chief of Staff better get his story straight because he told me (a contradictory story)." Dementia or overworked, the man plainly lied. He committed perjury over and over again without suffering any consequences. Dr. Chief of Staff still holds his same position at Facility by the River Health Care System, unscathed.

The deputy chief of staff testified to the group that I provided substandard care. He falsely stated that he reviewed all of the opioid cases involved personally. In reality, he gave the charts to be reviewed to his nonclinical administrative officer to review and she passed them off to a nonclinical secretary. The summary prepared by the nonclinical staff member proved nonsensical at best. The secretary told me about the situation, knowing she was put in a role she was not qualified to accept. This same deputy chief of staff fully supported me during Professional Standards Board meetings. He telephoned me at home to beg me to return because I was "so good at my job." Obviously, the enemy bit his Achilles heel and he succumbed to the conniving direction by the director and his side kick, the chief of staff. Whichever way the wind blows....

CHAPTER 13

The Testimonies the Ignorant Oversight Body (IOB) Liked to Ignore

> There are six things that the Lord hates, seven
> that are an abomination to him: haughty eyes, a
> lying tongue, and hands that shed innocent blood,
> a heart that devises wicked plans, feet that make
> haste to run to evil, a false witness who breathes out
> lies, and one who sows discord among brothers.
> —Proverbs 6:16–19 (ESV)

One of our service chiefs provided testimony that the director did not seem to like providers very much. She was right on the mark with her statement. She stated the new director "appears less physician friendly or supportive. He appears more business-like, if you will." She was kind. She elaborated stating in her thirty years of practicing medicine along with many years as a chief of staff for a 550-bed hospital and over 950 physicians, she stated, "this is the most egregious use of a summary suspension of privileges I have ever seen in my career. Totally and absolutely egregious." She inquired as to why didn't anyone ask me to stop the way I tapered opioids if anyone had a concern. She stated, "She would have stopped in a minute."

One of the investigators asked one of the primary care physicians if she was aware of the chief of staff directing physicians to prescribe medications that they were uncomfortable prescribing. The investigators ignored her validating reply.

Another primary care provider testified. I smiled as I read her testimony with a sense of pride, the good kind if good pride even exists. She informed the investigators that the chief of staff would approach her and other providers to write opioid prescriptions they did not support. She mentioned that I provided interference and took a lot of the chief of staff visits away from the providers. Once I left, the undesired attention by the chief of staff and his requests regarding opioid prescribing increased her apprehension and she left primary care.

A third primary care provider stated she was strong enough to say, "No" when the chief of staff approached her, but that others were not.

A neurologist stated the providers were not comfortable re-writing high dose valium prescriptions (another dangerous controlled substance, a benzodiazepine).

It became clear to me that these truthful clinical testimonies did not meet the need, the need to give Congress a goat. Over and over again, the clinical providers provided testimony that disproved the Ignorant Oversight Body's original conclusions that I practiced unsafe medicine related to opioids. The clinical providers substantiated that the chief of staff approached them to change opioid prescriptions. One testified that she thought the chief of staff's actions were illegal. The IOB ignored truthful testimony and it appeared that their actions were intentional and self-serving. Additionally, reporting the truth would require the IOB to admit they errored on their first report. Since members of Congress acted on the first IOB report, this would require these political persons to apologize. Apologizing would be too embarrassing for all of the elite leaders and possibly jeopardize their careers. As a consequence, the IOB continued their second investigation without amending their original faulty report. The chief of staff became the group's next goat.

CHAPTER 14

The 8,005-Page Data Dump
Received on the Day Before Pretrial

My soul clings to You; Your right hand upholds me.
—Psalm 63:8 (ESV)

To my disbelief and amazement, my attorney received an 8,005-page data dump the day before our pretrial hearing with the judge. Someone had to review the information and I accepted the challenge, producing a summary document for my attorney to review.

I learned my private email account had been hacked. The agency produced documents linked only to my private email account. Personal statements I sent to the Equal Rights Organization, Hassle Free Office, Complaint Department Office, Grievance Division Office, and Subcommittee on Oversight and Investigation stood out amongst the thousands of pages in plain sight. Nothing was sacred. I did not fear the discovery of the documents since I strived to always remain professional, forthright, and transparent with any form of communication. I used my private email appropriately in my opinion. I did not send patient information. I simply responded to questions imposed by investigating bodies under their direction.

I located communication about release of my photograph to the news station; a conversation with the chief of staff, the director, and another employee with her concerns about the number of patients on opioids.

The agency added fillers to the data dump with the intention of slowing us down and running up my legal fees no doubt. I had the time to filter the information myself, so although the process was time consuming and irritating, it didn't cost me a dime. Fillers included documents unrelated to the case, often repeated throughout the data dump. Topics about gastrointestinal fecal occult blood testing, neurology briefings, pharmacy report briefings, primary care resource guides for leaders, access guides, systems redesign training opportunities, emergency plans for the facility, view alert recommendations, women's health guidelines, and scheduling guidelines were included repetitively.

Pertinent documents were sandwiched in between the unrelated documents. To my delight and quite frankly surprise, buried gems popped up which proved helpful to my case. Important findings included an Ignorant Oversight Body action plan I prepared for the facility several months prior to the date of my summary suspension of privileges. The facility senior leaders used this Ignorant Oversight Body report as the reason they took action to remove my privileges citing unsafe medical practices. In reality, the leaders previously asked me to respond to the report. This was the report the chief of staff informed the Professional Standards Board members, which included me at the time, that he thought contained many errors. This is the report the PSB members requested for review and the chief of staff chose to ignore this request knowing the content contained misinterpretations. The twistedness of the story and timeline dumbfounded most of us for an extended period of time; but as I reviewed the hidden gems, I realized their justification of their unfair actions could be proven to be garbage. My action plan response to the IOB occurred months earlier. Why did the leaders not discipline me months earlier if I practiced unsafe medicine? Why was I asked by the quality management team of the facility, operating under the director, to prepare the action plan in response to the IOB report? As the medical expert, the quality management team tasked me with the response. The director's action to suspend my privileges was nothing short of retaliation in response to whistleblowing about unsafe opioid practices and airing of the news story on television.

Another gem shined into view. The quality management nurse sent an electronic message to the regional office to inform them of the television news story. Regional leaders immediately responded requesting an urgent response from the chief of staff. I knew about many of the regional and headquarters email strings because I was on the communication. However, I learned about the frantic communications days later when I returned from a two week leave following recertification of my family practice certificate and interviewing for a new position at a different large health care system facility. Discussions took place in my absence. Obviously, in my absence, the leaders plotted against me and I became their scapegoat politically.

Senior facility leaders and regional leaders relied on my expertise regarding opioid safety. Through many years of experience, they labeled me as an opioid safety expert witness. I located responses by the chief of staff to the Legal National Office that internal medicine and family practice physicians are considered to be the "specialists who provide pain management services" at our facility. The chief of pharmacy identified me as the facility's prescription drug monitoring program point of contact for pharmacy and the facility in general. A pharmacy manager and I responded to regional inquiries about pain management and opioid safety action plans. As I previously stated, quality management leaders tasked me with providing the IOB action plan related to opioid safety.

The data dump included documents reflecting the importance of patient satisfaction scores. A special report created by headquarters ranked all of the facilities across the country in multiple categories. The categories included quality of care goals such as mortality percentages, care complications, length of hospital stay, readmission rates, chronic care quality measures, and more. Patient satisfaction, efficiency and physician capacity measurements also appeared on the report. Our facility earned many stars for quality measures. Overall, we ranked just fine in comparison to other facilities. Ranking outcomes per number of facilities were: care transition 16 out of 146; employee satisfaction 17 out of 146, performance measures 18 out of 146, mortality 19 out of 129. But "five-star Rick" as the director was mockingly called, focused on the one area we failed to shine, patient satisfaction, and if he did not put all of the blame on me personally, I would have understood his frustration because Facility by the River

Health Care System ranked 125 out of 146 facilities. Implementation of opioid safety initiatives had a lot to do with patient satisfaction. Holding patients accountable for safely using their opioids angered the patients who lost their income selling their opioids. When prescriptions were no longer given to patients who combined opioids with illegal substances, visited multiple physicians for multiple prescriptions and filled prescriptions at multiple locations, overdosed on their opioids, or developed medical diseases prohibiting the use of opioids for chronic pain, they became angry and complained. Instead of being embarrassed by their illegal actions or grateful that providers were preventing unintentional overdoses and death, the patients complained. The patients' complaints infuriated five-star Rick. The director frequently redirected his anger toward me, publicly. I endured the harassment in the name of patient safety...for a time.

While opioid safety initiative implementation influenced patient satisfaction, other factors outside of my control entered into the scoring system too. Our facility was old and dilapidated. Patients could not find parking spots and lack of parking spots led to them being late for appointments, frustrating the medical staff. Physician turnover and lack of primary care physicians interfered with patient satisfaction also. Our primary care service team overcame these obstacles, filling all of the vacancies in primary care, increasing employee satisfaction resulting in our facility being one of the most improved and recognized nationally. Over time, our primary care service employees felt supported and the burden from being over-paneled, having to see too many patients in a day from lack of providers, slowly faded as we retained providers and hired new physicians. We could all breathe again.

Other factors entered into decreased patient satisfaction that could not be controlled such as ethnicity or gender of the employees. Some patients held onto prejudice that we strove to eliminate. Specialty wait times increased and outsourcing of care failed as a solution because the facility failed to pay for services provided in the community in a timely manner or at all. The community opportunities stopped. Specialty wait times grew.

Patients also did not get to choose where they received community care. Many patients traveled two or four hours to see a specialist in our state. Sometimes the travel proved fruitful; but other times the travel proved wasteful. Many other factors leading to poor patient satisfaction scores no doubt existed beyond our team's knowledge. These are just a few of the complaints our team understood as obstacles.

Multiple investigators visited Facility by the River Health Care System in response to opioid safety concerns reported to the groups. The data dump included valuable documentation of the visits. Not only was I concerned about opioid safety at our facility, large investigative bodies took notice too. Unfortunately, these investigators relied on interviews with senior leaders. Although the groups interviewed clinicians who reported significant concerns about the director and chief of staff interfering with opioid prescribing, the groups ignored these responses. To my delight, the facility most likely unknowingly included clinicians' and senior leaders' transcripts. Jackpot!

The year prior, I traveled with a fellow Veteran to a conference as access champions for our facility. I appreciated this young man's willingness to steer our travel and assist me in the new process. Motivated to climb the ladder of success, he volunteered to assist our facility with all of his ambition and I admired him at the time. When five-star Rick arrived, the two Army buddies bonded and I became the joke of the week. I separated myself from them and my Air Force Veteran administrative officer accepted the challenge of negotiating bombs thrown at us related to access. I stepped aside and praised his efforts. As I sorted through the mile-high piled data documents, I stumbled upon the proof of my suspicions about the young man on page 6,452. Mr. Access stated that he was sick of me advocating for primary care. There it was in black and white, plain as day. Mr. Access despised me even though he was valued and respectfully included in all of our rapid performance work group projects related to access, sharing our success. I pitied the fool.

I found documents the facility obtained but were not entitled to legally such as documents I sent to the Equal Rights Organization. I found my timeline from my private email account to the investigator along with my hotline report and letter. I didn't mind the facility having this information because the information contained everything that I had previously reported to the facility leaders; but the manner which they received the documents was unethical and most likely illegal. They included email messages I sent to the Complaint Department Office from my private account. I forgot about those messages. I laughed. I sure was busy.

Just after laughing, I became still. Personal statements I sent under my private email pertaining to unwanted press and media attention stood out blatantly. The press and media painted me as a villain and I was forced to sit back and endure the humiliation. I remembered, "be still and know that I am God." I remained still for quite some time.

CHAPTER 15
Disclosures

Because of the LORD's great love we are not consumed, for His compassions never fail.
                    —Lamentations 3:22 (NIV)

The evidence I supplied to my attorney supporting my attempts to save lives painted a clear picture of the unfortunate neglect by senior leaders at our facility choosing patient satisfaction over saving lives and politicians choosing votes over lives.

Exhibits
Context Descriptions of Sample Oral Disclosures

Christmas 2015

On or about Christmas 2015, Dr. Sky reports concern about a patient to Dr. COS about this employee's excessive visits to the Urgent Care as well as excessive contact with the PC providers, other PC staff for more opioids. Later, Dr. Sky reports to police about her concerns and this situation is investigated. Much later, this employee seeks help for addiction and is admitted for substance abuse help.

New Year 2016

Dr. Sky informs Dr. Chief of Staff that she will be reporting diversion cases to the police. He agreed.

Dr. Sky informs Dr. Chief of Staff that another patient and employee was inappropriately negative on UDS for amphetamine and the patient was filling Adderall (amphetamine) and was 92 tabs short for pill count. He was receiving hydrocodone also. This is a patient of Dr. PCP.

Dr. Sky discusses a patient with Dr. COS and informs him that the patient is harassing people as a drug seeker.

Spring 2016

Dr. Sky informs Dr. COS of a patient picketing at the facility. Dr. Sky told Dr. COS that the patient filled 720 tabs of hydrocodone and 180 tabs of tramadol in the community on Summer 2019 and 240 tabs of hydrocodone at the facility the next month. This patient averaged filling 300 tabs of opioid per month from the community. A taper was suggested by Dr. Sky to Dr. COS. PCP, NP had a good note of explanation in the chart. Narcotic agreements were signed by the patient on four occasions. He has written many letters to Congress which have been researched by primary care administrative staff. He is still active as of the summer of 2017.

Dr. Sky discusses the same patient with Dr. COS and report from PCP, NP in follow up from a group meeting to discuss a different patient which took place and included Mr. Suicide Prevention Coordinator, Mr. Chief of Police, Dr. Pain Psychologist, Dr. Sky, Dr. Mental Health, Ms. Suicide Prevention Coordinator. It was mentioned that two hours of time were spent on the phone with the patient by Mr. Suicide Prevention Coordinator. The group initiated a plan for follow up. Note that the patient is still very active through Congress and others including Dr. COS as of the summer of 2017.

Dr. COS and Dr. Sky met to discuss the culture regarding opioid safety. Dr. Sky requests we give a consistent message to patients. She discussed how time-consuming entertaining complaints around opioid use and chronic pain with Dr. COS. Patients complain to the clinic team, patient advocates, chief of staff office, director's office, Congress, and the President. Dr. Sky mentions receiving support from Dr. Pain Psychologist, Mr. Chief of Police, Mr. and Ms. Suicide Prevention Coordinators. She requests having a round table discussion with key players.

Summer 2016

Dr. Sky reviews concerns regarding a previous patient and employee with Dr. COS.

Dr. COS met with Dr. Sky, Ms. Patient Advocate leader, Ms. Nursing leader to discuss interactions between PC and patient advocates. Dr. Sky requested patient advocates not ask to change opioid safety plans or comment on the number of opioids dispensed to patients. This really is to be determined by clinical staff, especially providers.

Dr. Sky received a call from Ms. PC RN requesting police presence in the front area of the lobby and she spoke with Mr. Chief of Police. Diversion concerns were also reported to Mr. Chief about drug dealing in the ED area. Mr. Chief of Police agreed to have these areas patrolled. There were not enough police to be stationed in the lobby or any certain area so they patrolled the areas. Mr. Chief of Police was very receptive to Dr. Sky's invitation to join the Opioid Safety Initiative Work Group and he has been a regular attender up to this date, summer of 2017. Dr. Sky informed Dr. COS of this discussion.

Dr. Sky, Dr. Chief of Staff, Ms. RN leader AO, primary care AOs met to discuss patient advocate concerns by PC. Dr. Sky asked that patient advocates not judge clinical decisions made by PCPs and Dr. Sky encouraged support of PCPs. Dr. Sky asked Dr. Chief of Staff, "who will write the prescription (opioid) if the COS approves reinstatement of opioids and the PCP is not in agreement?" This is an ongoing ethical dilemma. Dr. Sky frequently states that another provider cannot force a provider to write for any prescription for which the provider is not in agreement. This pertains to multiple discussions about having a multidisciplinary group meet to decide what should be done as a team. Dr. Sky states that unless the prescribing provider is included in the discussion and agrees, it is not ethical or lawful to coerce a provider to write for a prescription he/she deems unethical, unlawful, or unsafe for the patient.

Dr. Sky learned that a patient died. He was found slumped in the stuck elevator. He was taking fentanyl 50mcg every 3 days and received 240 oxycodone tabs regularly. Dr. Sky reported this information to Dr. Chief of Staff and Dr. Lab Chief and Chair of Ethics Committee.

Dr. Chief of Staff discusses use of acupuncture as an alternative treatment for pain with Dr. Sky. A previous patient is discussed with Dr. Sky. Dr. COS approved transfer of this difficult opioid seeking patient to a different rural clinic. Dr. Sky reinforced the need to taper the patient off of opioids for her safety. The patient is very active with Congress with interference by Dr. COS intermittently and regularly up to this point in time in the summer of 2017.

Fall 2016

Dr. Sky met with Mr. Director and Dr. Chief of Staff on or about Mr. Director's first month on the job, fall of 2016, to brief him on the opioid problems at FBTRHCS including over-prescribing of opioids, patient drug seeking and diversion, and lack of training in urine drug screens.

A previously discussed patient received approval by the COS to relocate to another rural clinic and this was upsetting to the original clinical staff because they worked with the patient to taper her off of opioids over an extended period of time. Dr. Sky discussed this with Dr. Chief of Staff. Dr. Chief of Staff and Dr. Sky also discussed goals to have not have any patients on greater than 400 morphine equivalents by late fall for chronic pain. Use of Dr. Clinical Pharmacy Specialist for tapering by a specialist would be encouraged. The morphine equivalent goal for the facility is to achieve no patients with chronic pain on greater than 100 morphine equivalents.

Winter 2016

Dr. Chief of Staff, Dr. Sky, Ms. Woman's Health Coordinator, Dr. Pain Psychologist met to discuss two patients regarding opioid use. A previous patient was discussed. Another previously mentioned patient was discussed. This patient went to the Director's office. She was scheduled for a one-hour appointment with a new provider. An earlier appointment was being requested. Many services were offered to the complaining patient such as a tens unit, RS4i medical device used to treat pain, amitriptyline and gabapentin medications with a plan to try Lyrica next if gabapentin was unsuccessful. Plans were made for further treatment options.

Winter 2016 and New Year 2017

Mr. Director attended FBTHRHCS's regularly scheduled primary care meetings in which Dr. Sky routinely updated him on opioid issues and repeatedly disclosed her concerns about how the medical center administration was pressuring primary care physicians to over-prescribe opioids, approving transfer requests by drug seeking patients, and allowing patient advocates to inappropriately dictate physician medical decisions.

Spring 2017

Dr. Sky informed Dr. Chief of Staff that she was told the Director ordered to have someone order marinol for a patient via Dr. Chief of Staff. Dr. Pain Psychologist Informed Dr. Sky that she met with the director to have this done.

Dr. Sky informed Dr. Chief of Staff that the group meetings for patients on opioids for chronic pain were not helpful. She reminded Dr. Chief of Staff that a group cannot tell a provider what he or she should order. The PCP would need to be in agreement to the plan. Dr. Sky stated she was concerned that the facility including Dr. Chief of Staff is heading in the wrong direction with patients with addiction. Marinol is now being used for one patient and Dr. Sky asked that this not be put onto primary care providers as an expectation.

These few disclosures provided a taste of the bountiful concerns reported to senior leaders and politicians on a regular basis by Dr. Sky and her supportive primary care team. Mr. Director and Dr. Chief of Staff looked the other way, took a blind eye to the reports, and swept serious concerns under the rug repeatedly, all in the name of self-seeking motives.

CHAPTER 16
Prayer Warriors

Do not be anxious about anything, but in every
situation, by prayer and petition, with thanksgiv-
ing, present your requests to God.
—Philippians 4:6 (NIV)

Understanding the strength of prayer, I started a prayer warrior text chain as we traveled to take on Goliath, the large health care system, with just a sling and a stone. An administrative judge was appointed as part of the Legal Battle Board process for whistleblowers. As I write "whistleblowers," I cringe. The name exudes a negative connotation. Be that as it may, the term is used and in reality, the connotation should reflect the bravery required by a warrior fighting injustice. The actual definition is a person who informs on a person or organization engaged in an illicit activity. I don't feel brave. Because of my insecurities, I lean on the Lord and ask for prayer from other Christians to uphold me, and rely on the Holy Spirit to lead me into battle, just like David. I am relying on the same outcome that David received, victory with glory to God.

This is dialog from our prayer warrior support chain:

Dear Brothers and Sisters in Christ, I am calling all of you to respectfully ask for your prayers. David and I are traveling to the river state for our day in court in the summer of 2018, in the fight for opioid safety for patients and those in communities surrounding the facility, especially in the river state. I ask that you pray that God be glorified in the outcome of this case above all. I have faith He will be with me and the Holy Spirit will guide my testimony. I trust God will reveal the truth about political influences obstructing medical facilities, especially providers, to apply much needed opioid safety initiatives to prevent unintentional overdoses that are plaguing our country. I believe in the power of prayer....so please pray for us, especially on our Legal Battle Board dates. Thank you to all of you who have been praying already and offering support. David and I are grateful for all of you!

Prayerfully, Big

The prayer warriors prayed and prayed...we were covered in prayer.

Bombarding every step with warring ministering angels on your behalf!

My prayers are with you for safe travels and for wisdom as you stand before these others and speak truth.

LORD GOD we thank you for your love and protection. Right now, we lift up Big and David for your protection and guidance as they step up in defense of those who serve and have served this nation and risked their lives to protect us. We ask that you put your shield around Big and David and give them the words to speak as they come and testify before this hearing...again we thank you that you are our Great Shepherd and pray that you be glorified in all that is said and done in this situation...in the precious Name of Christ Jesus we pray...AMEN.

Amen and amen to these prayers. May you carry with you the spirit of David in slaying this Goliath. You are fearless, my faithful friend. Prayers are with you both and with all who cross your path and we are blessed for you both...:)

Our prayers are with Big and David as they battle against the injustice to the system and to the patients!

I will light a candle and say a prayer for you today
at church.

Psalms 121…Amen…God bless.

Philippians 4:4–7

David and Big, we pray the love of the Lord shine through you at this meeting. Pray also that God be Glorified and His Spirit will go forth and touch those in need of His free gift of salvation…God bless, you guys.

Praying for you both as you go forth today.

This was my verse of the day: "Fear thou not; for I am with thee." This was my verse of the day!

"I can do all things through Him who strengthens me" (Phil. 4:13). As His messenger, He will provide you with the wisdom and strength to make the truth shine through.

Big and David…holding you both close to my heart and in my prayers. Things happen for reason. And as hard as this has been on you and David, I believe God chose you as the perfect person to take care of this. He needed someone who is clear on what is right and is willing to fight to uphold. Big, your faith, perseverance, honesty, and integrity are just a few of the amazing qualities you possess that will see you through. Also know your friends and family are with you too. Love you!

Praying everything went good today. Do you testify again tomorrow? God's continued grace and blessings on you both.

Lord, You told us if we do actually command you call us your friends. Be with your friend today.

"Blessed be the LORD, Because He has heard the voice of my supplications! The LORD is my strength and my shield; My heart trusted in Him, and I am helped; Therefore my heart greatly rejoices, And with my song I will praise Him. The LORD is their strength, And He is the saving refuge of His anointed. Save Your people, And bless Your inheritance; Shepherd them also, And bear them up forever. (Psalms 28:6–9)

God is good. All the time!

Thank you all for your prayers and support. One more day! I sure feel the benefits from all of the prayers. I know what peace beyond understanding feels like! Praise be to God!

Big, hope all went well today. May all these prayers be with you tomorrow. Love, Dad

Hi, Big! So good to hear that our prayers are working. What time tomorrow is your testimony so we all can pray extra at that time?

Dear Lord. I lift up Big, James, and David today. May you go before them down the path you have given

I will be travailing in prayer for the next hour 7:30–8:30 a.m. for the "Light of truth to SET THE CAPTIVES FREE."

Hang in there you are stronger than you think.

Holy cow! That is very intense. I can't imagine what you are going through! I am with you & know that I am praying.

Keeping you close in thought, heart & prayers.

Be not dismayed; for I am thy God: I will strengthen thee; yea, I will uphold thee with the right hand of my righteousness." (Isaiah 41:10, KJV)

The prayer warriors prayers comforted David and me. When I grew weary and anxious, I read their prayers and felt at peace. I knew I was covered in righteous prayer and in God's will.

CHAPTER 17
The Prehearing Meeting

Be thou prepared, and prepare for thyself, thou,
and all thy company that are assembled unto
thee, and be thou a guard unto them.
—Ezekiel 38:7 (KJV)

My attorney prepared an organized list of questions for me to answer as a witness at the hearing centered around the following topics: background, opioids, backlash, pressure on the primary care providers to prescribe opioids, disclosures, illegal and dangerous activity, Ignorant Oversight Body report, retaliation from the television news story, retaliation and the suspension of privileges, investigations during the suspension of privileges, retaliation and removal from opioid champion role, reinstatement of privileges, proposed reprimand, leave and housekeeping items, retaliation and the East Coast Medical Center offer, damages and retirement, financial damages, reputational damages, and emotional damages.

The background questions painted a backdrop to the case and focused on my professional training, military service, career at the large health care system, reasons I became a physician, duties as a leader at the three facility locations, responsibilities of my appointments, supervisor names and performance ratings. The opioid questions established me as an expert opioid safety witness as I was asked to outline my training and experiences, referencing exhibits. The questioning clearly reflected that nobody else at the Facility by the River Health Care System had similar opioid safety training and experience as a provider or a leader. I thank God daily for providing the perfect attorney, above and beyond anyone I ever expected. I hadn't thought much about being an opioid safety expert. I knew this fight to save lives during the opioid epidemic was my passion and I immersed myself in education, training, and application of opioid safety initiatives. The witness questions provoked responses to when it is safe, unsafe, lawful, and unlawful to prescribe opioids for chronic pain. I defined terms such as weaning, tapering, suspending in relation to prescriptions.

My attorney asked me questions about the large health care system's role and facility's role in addressing the national epidemic. Lastly, turning to exhibits, he asked me how Facility by the River Health Care System compared to other facilities across the nation. He asked me to comment on the exhibit reflecting our community's unintentional overdose and death rate. The problem at FBTRHCS became clear. By choosing patient satisfaction over safety, people were overdosing and dying at an alarming rate.

CHAPTER 18
Direct Examination

Fear thou not; for I am with the: be not dismayed; for I am thy God: I will strengthen thee; yea, I will help thee: yea, I will uphold thee with the right hand of my righteousness.
—Isaiah 41:10 (KJV)

David and I departed for the river city in the early summer of 2018. Our day in court was materializing before us in less than a week. I felt my stomach in my throat. I prayed to God to give me the strength and courage to press on in His glory. Amen.

The driving trip clocked in at forty-eight hours overall, so we took our time on this journey toward justice. I don't like to fly if I don't have to so we planned a visit to the great lakes area afterward to recuperate with supportive family and friends. We stopped overnight in the badlands and the following night in the land of cornfields and soybeans. Somehow, this comforted me. We completed the last leg of the journey to the river city and found a pleasant and bright hotel which would be our place of refuge for three nights.

Following a good night's sleep which was a miracle in itself, we arose early and found our favorite Dunkin Donuts coffee spot. Oh, how I missed Dunkin Donuts coffee. Familiarity helped calm my nerves. We drove to the annex of the Facility by the River Health Care System, the location of the hearing. The judge resided in Chicago and we videoed in for the hearing from a small conference room in the annex of the hospital. The annex location proved to be perfect. Many of my dear friends and colleagues worked in this building. My Zumba buddies and I danced in this building, the good that came out of the bad of working at this facility. When I walked into the annex, I spotted a dear sister in Christ. We beamed with delight when we embraced. God sent me support. The police officer who let me into the facility smiled warmly. Did he know why I was there? I reunited with other close colleagues during the visit to my previous workplace. I believe God truly put each person in my path over those long days.

After finding the conference room, David and I realized we were early. We waited. David dressed casually. We believed I would be the only one allowed in the room. David could have stayed in the end; but he felt he was dressed inappropriately and we both agreed I may testify better if he was not present for what reason we thought this I am uncertain. After a long wait, I met Max for the first time in person. He brought another polished attorney with him to help navigate the hearing. Financially, the law firm provided me with a bargain to have two attorneys which I appreciated immensely. The two attorneys proved worthy of every penny. Max was amazingly prepared. Everyone could appreciate his preparedness. My face beamed like a proud mother gazing at her successful brilliant son. I thanked God for allowing Max to be my attorney. William knew how to set traps. Traps that snared liars. I did not see this quality initially. I wondered if William knew my case at all. He did not appear to be prepared. All of that doubt vanished as the trial proceeded. William's value became evident during the enemies' testimonies. He also provided support for Max, less experienced in court. They confided in one another continuously, plotting and planning. Long periods of silence would creep in while they collaborated; but I learned to stay silent and trust in their expertise.

I testified first. As the time to begin approached, I felt terrified. I prayed. I usually do well in front of crowds and I had much practice with public speaking due to all of my previous training and job duties. This situation proved to be different. I prayed again and again for strength, courage, God's will to be done, and that I would not faint. I am a big fainter during times of illness, pain, and extreme fear. I did not faint.

I sat at the head of the table, facing the judge on the screen. My two attorneys sat to my right and the facility's attorneys perched to my left with the meeting coordinator running the equipment. The judge appeared fair. I thanked God. You just never know in these situations. He had a stenographer with him. Introductions occurred and the judge asked me to raise my right hand. My day in court began.

Mr. Attorney:

Q   What is your name?
A   Dr. B. Sky
Q   So, how long have you been a physician?
A   Twenty-four years
Q   And what made you want to become a doctor?
A   I was very affected as a child about the Vietnam War and I always wanted to care for those war Veterans.
Q   What was your position at FBTRHCS?
A   I was the associate chief of staff (ACOS) for primary care. And I was also the opioid safety initiative champion for the facility.
Q   Just for an acronym, what's ACOS?
A   ACOS, associate chief of staff.
Q   All right, and were the positions you supervised all at one facility or at more than one.
A   They were at more than one.
Q   And what were all of those facilities?
A   City 1, 2, 3, 4, 5, 6
Q   And how did you come to be the ACOS at FBTRHCS?
A   I was actually recruited based upon my experience in leadership and then also for my opioid safety experience.
Q   And what exactly were your duties?
A   I oversaw the primary care department on basically the daily operations with other administrative staff. I was in charge of hiring primary care providers and supervision. Credentialing and privileging, reviewing medical records for each provider,

watching quality measures, safety issues, and things that go with running a primary care department.

Q   And how much of your own clinical judgement did you bring to managing the primary care team?

A   I used clinical judgment every day. It was essential for my position.

Q   What are the ways you used clinical judgment?

A   I did a lot of chart reviews and quality reviews, and you have to understand medicine to perform these reviews. Also, with hiring and staffing, I needed to have medical knowledge to ask the right questions in reviewing an applicant's qualifications. In credentialing and privileging, medical education is necessary to award or deny privileges.

Q   And would you have been able to do your job without those privileges?

A   No. It is an absolute requirement to have medical privileges.

Q   And how often did you work with patients directly?

A   I did not work directly face-to-face with patients very much other than filling in.

Q   So, what were your responsibilities in interacting with the medical center's upper level leadership?

A   That is very much what I did. We worked with the executives and the leadership team to the clinical staff, and I interacted with them really every day. I reported weekly to the executive team about our primary care service line and I reported monthly to the executive team regarding pain management and opioid safety. I attended clinical executive board committee meetings which incorporated the executive leadership team and peer review quality committee with the executive board in attendance.

Q   So, who is your first line supervisor?

A   Dr. Chief of Staff

Q   So, who was your second line supervisor?

A   Mr. Director as of the fall of 2016. Prior to that we had acting directors float.

Q   And how were your performance ratings?

A   Outstanding.

Q   And would you please go to exhibit—

A   And are they right before me here?

Q   Yes, it's the binder.

A   Okay.

Q   This is Exhibit B of Appellant's pre-hearing submissions.

Q   And what is this exhibit?

A   This is a mid-term proficiency rating mid-year from fiscal year 2017 and I got rated in the spring of 2017 by Dr. Chief of Staff

Q   And what was your rating on this proficiency?

A   It's checked here and it says fully successful or better.

Q   So, Dr. Sky, are you familiar with this exhibit?

A   Yes.

Q   What is it?

A   This is the fiscal year '16 proficiency rating.

Q   And, what was your rating on this document?

A   Outstanding.

Q   And would you please go to the second to last page and last page of the document. And could you please read the comments there?

A   Dr. Sky has performed in an exemplary manner. She has worked tirelessly in support of her primary care providers, as well as assisting in work groups, performance improvement efforts, and committees. She has the confidence of her providers and their respect. She maintains a passion of ensuring patients have the best care experience. Dr. Sky has characterized herself as an effective and highly-regarded leader in managing a complex service line. She is a strong asset to the organization. Dr. Chief of Staff

Q   What were your responsibilities regarding opioid initiatives?

A   I was the Opioid Safety Co-champion along with Dr. Psychologist.

Q   What did it mean to be a co-champion?

A   I was considered the expert that others would go to with any opioid safety initiative questions. I had extensive training in the past and fifteen years of experience, and so I was elected to be the champion. And, when anybody in the facility had questions such as a pharmacist, mental health provider, social worker, primary care provider, leader, nurse, or others, he or she would contact me for advice and recommendations.

Q Did you have any special expertise regarding opioids?

A Yes.

Q And, what as that?

A I had, like I said, 15 years of experience with opioid safety. I was on the ground floor nationally with the organization working with Great Lakes Medical Center, who is now considered a champion facility for opioid safety. I worked with them as part of a multi-disciplinary group for eight years where we would present difficult cases and make decisions as a group. From there I got into leadership and I was recruited by a facility in the land of corn and soybeans and pain management actually came under my service line. I was the primary and specialty care service line director at that time.

So, we spent three years actually as a team, a team of mental health providers and physiatrists. We had primary care staff, social workers, nursing, and executives working together to develop a fully functioning pain clinic under primary and specialty care leadership in which I was the service line leader. We incorporated acupuncture, chiropractic care, pain psychologists, physiatrists, interventionalists. It was a fully functional pain clinic. It was very successful.

Q And are you familiar with this exhibit?

A Yes.

Q And what are the documents in this exhibit?

A These are some examples of some training certificates. They're from different continuing medical education courses on opioid safety and pain management I attended.

Q And what kind of training do these certificates represent?

A Opioid training, pain management training.

Q So, what did you know that any doctor authorized by law to prescribe opioids would not necessarily know?

153

A   I knew a lot about safety monitoring such as how to use the state prescription monitoring program, how to interpret urine drug screens, how to use pill counts for monitoring, and other safety interventions. I understood different interactions with medications, what morphine equivalents we should be using, and interactions of opioids with different health concerns such as what would cause respiratory depression or sedation.

Q   Did any of the other physicians at FBTRHCS have equivalent opioid training to yours?

A   No.

Q   So did the physicians at FBTRHCS come to ask you questions about opioid practice?

A   Yes.

Q   Did that include senior positions?

A   Yes.

Q   Did Dr. Chief of Staff ask you questions about opioids?

A   Yes.

Q   Did Dr. Deputy Chief of Staff ask you questions about opioids?

A   Yes.

Q   What are the dangers to the individual patient being prescribed long-term opioid therapy?

A   The main danger is unintentional overdose which includes death, but there are other dangers. When patients are on opioids, they're at increased risk for car crashes, similar to alcohol intoxication. They are at risk for falling, especially in the elderly, because opioids are sedating.

There's risk for respiratory depression or a decrease in breathing, especially if they have obstructive sleep apnea and they are not using their CPAP machines. If patients have chronic obstructive pulmonary disease, they are at risk for having respiratory depression. Elderly patients often have metabolism problems, kidney disease, or liver disease. The effects of opioids in these patients are accentuated and prolonged making prescribing opioids for elderly patients concerning.

Q   So, what are the warning signs doctors use to know when it is dangerous or improper to prescribe opioids to a particular patient?

A   Well, if patients present and look like they are having trouble breathing, you know there might be a problem. If they have an addiction history, we apply established criteria to assess safety and risk of opioid use. Any addiction history, including tobacco, which many providers forget about, increases the risk in using opioids. Tobacco, alcohol, other street drug addictions increase the risk for dependence and addiction if opioids are used.

Q   So, what do you use for the prescription of opioids by the hospital after the—

A   Well, the risks for the community come with any patient that is getting a certain number of pills per month, and when we check the drug screen, if there's nothing in the urine, we worry about diversion.

Q   What is diversion?

A   Diversion means the person is either intentionally selling the drug, or the patient's opioids are being accessed by others as in stealing the medication. People look in other people's medicine cabinets and the medication gets out in the community. Unintentional overdose can be the outcome and possibly death.

Q   Are opioids addictive?

A   Yes.

Q   How addictive are they?

A   In some people, it only takes one dose. If they take an opioid after surgery, they can potentially get addicted on the first dose, and we do not know who has this tendency and who doesn't. But studies are now coming out and show that if somebody uses opioids over seven days, the likelihood of addiction increases.

Q   So, what is the best way of getting patients off of opioids?

A   There are different processes for getting people off of opioids. If they are taking them regularly and they're on a really high dose or high pill count load, we do what's called a taper. A taper or a reduction in dose over time. There are two forms of tapers. There's a rapid taper if you are worried about the patient such as someone having trouble breathing, you can decrease the dose by twenty to fifty percent per day if you have to. And if you are not worried about the patient, then you can go slower and gradually reduce the dose by twenty to fifty percent per week to get them either to a safer level or get them completely off of opioids.

Q   Yes, what does weaning mean in the context of opioids?

A   I equate weaning to tapering. And that is to slowly take them off or reduce the dose of the medication.

Q   And what does suspending mean?

A   Suspending means not filling. And, do you want to know when it's used or does that answer the question?

Q   Sure.

A   Usually a suspension or not filling is when you find that either the patient says they are no longer taking the medication, so you would not renew it, or that if there is no drug in the urine and they are filling the medication on time monthly, you would not refill the medication. You would be concerned about diversion.

Q   Why would you be concerned about diversion if there is nothing in the urine?

A   If no drug is in the urine, it means they are not ingesting the medication.

Q   Are there other terms we should know the definitions of?

A   Stopping or terminating medications, not renewing, those types of terms.

Q   Are there any situations when it is appropriate to wean a patient?

A   Yes, if they appear sedated, the dose is probably too high and if they are acting incoherently, you would want to decrease the dose. If they've used the medication for a suicide attempt or an unintentional overdose, we would wean them off the medication because using the medication is extremely dangerous. And then again, I think I've described the different health situations unless you want me to say it again.

Q   No. And what about if you find other illegal drugs?

A   Yes, that would be found on the urine drug screen. We do check for other illegal drugs such as cocaine, methamphetamine, and other illegal substances.

Q   So, when should patients be kept on long-term opioid therapy indefinitely?

A   The only time this is okay indefinitely is with hospice patients. Otherwise, it's really an individual evaluation and it's not really encouraged to keep people on opioids chronically anymore.

Q   Is it ever appropriate to increase a patient's opioid dose?

A   Yes, for hospice patients to keep them comfortable.

Q   Are there dangers associated with weaning patients off of long-term opioids too quickly?

A   In weaning patients off of opioids, there is no risk of dying. That is something people need to be made aware. It's different for benzodiazepines but we are talking opioids here. You do have to go slow on benzodiazepines, but for opioids, they might get uncomfortable for up to a week or so, but they cannot die. We provide what is called a comfort pack of medication, it is not opioid medication, it's pills and different substances to help with diarrhea and other uncomfortable side effects.

Q   When a patient has been over-prescribed opioids by a prior physician, is it dangerous to keep that prior level of opioids in place?

A   Yes. If you are covering for a provider or take over somebody's panel of patients and the doses are really high, you need to question this practice.

Q   In general, how do the risks of keeping a patient on a high opioid dose compare to risks of tapering?

A   If you keep them on a high dose and you are concerned about them dying, every day they take that medication, it is a risk that they could die. Tapering quickly, you cannot die. It is safer to taper when faced with this concern.

     It is much better to choose tapering than risking unintentional overdose and dying from a high dose of opioid medication.

Q   When is suspending a patient's opioid prescription immediately appropriate?

A   If the patient is no longer taking the medication, we suspend it or discontinue it. Also, if we check the urine drug screen and we confirm there is no drug in the urine, then we would not renew the medication. We would suspend the prescription.

Q   Is it illegal to prescribe opioids outside of the proper scope of verification?

A   Yes.

Q   What kind of prescriptions of opioids are appropriate enough
to be considered illegal?

A   If the provider gives opioids to somebody when you know that
there is no drug in the urine, then it is illegal. You are basically
being a supplier for a suspected diversion. The patient could be
stockpiling the medication; but the typical thing if nothing is in
the urine is that they are not ingesting the medication and the
provider must suspect diversion.

Also, if a prescriber gives opioid medication to somebody
that you know is actively doing methamphetamine or cocaine,
the provider would not give the patient opioid medication in
that instance either. It is a very dangerous combination and the
action would be very concerning.

Q   Can physicians have their licenses taken away for mis-prescribing opioids?

A   Yes.

Q   And can physicians be criminally liable for mis-prescribing
opioids?

A   Yes.

Q   It is okay for one physician to order another to prescribe opioids?

A   No.

Q   Why not?

A   Each physician is responsible to protect his or her medical
license, and there is a relationship that a physician develops
with the patient. And to order somebody to do something that
the primary care provider in this case doesn't think is correct, to
me is very much coercion and an illegal activity.

Q   Why is it illegal?

A   The primary care provider, as in this case, knows the patient,
they have a relationship, the provider knows the medical record.
And the provider knows what is going on clinically. The person ordering the physician does not know the patient, does not
know the medical record, any drug interactions, patient history,
social history, and other clinical information. And nor can the
primary care provider reveal confidential information. Thus, it

becomes very dangerous to have somebody order a physician to write a prescription.

Q   Is it okay for a non-physician to direct a physician to prescribe opioids?

A   No.

Q   What was the organization's guidance on reducing long-term opioid prescriptions?

A   Initially they were going for getting everybody that is over 200 morphine equivalents down below 200 morphine equivalent daily dose. And then the goal was to taper to below 100. They used the Center for Disease Control guidelines. We followed those guidelines in detail. And those guidelines encouraged going below 50 morphine equivalents.

Q   And when you came to FBTRHCS, what was your impression of how the medical center was handling opioid prescriptions?

A   The good things they were doing was they were getting the pain agreements, it's like a contract between the patient and the provider. They were good about signing the agreements and getting them in the patients' charts.

However, they were not good at enforcing the breach of the agreements. Also, the facility was good at getting urine drug screens done. They were actually leaders in the region, but they did not act on the results of the urine drug screen. Partially this was because the physicians did not understand how to interpret the urine drug screens. There was a lot of confusion on urine drug screen results. However, the providers did not act on inappropriately negative urine drug screens for example. This means that the urine did not have the opioid in the urine and the opioid should have been in the urine if the patient was ingesting the medication.

Q   Did FBTRHCS as a region have a problem with opioids?

A   Yes, especially one city where we have a hospital had one of the highest overdose rates in the country. So, that was a concern that we had heard from facilities there, and that included primary care. That fact was very much a concern.

Q   What did you do to improve FBTRHCS' opioid management rates?

A   Oh, I became very active. We had an opioid safety initiative work group, and I became the leader of that work group. I was on the pain management committee also. The primary care providers did all the prescribing for the opioids and I was their supervisor so, not only did I oversee them on the other aspects of primary care, I also was the go-to person for the primary care providers, as well as the pharmacists, the techs that had questions, mental health providers, social workers, and others such as nurses.

     I also helped to educate the entire clinical medical staff. We had weekly medical staff meetings which I'd often provide a section of education and Dr. Psychologist did the management psychology side of things.

     We went around to different groups such as the patient advocates, primary care providers, mental health providers, ER physicians and educated them.

Q   And what effect did all of that have on the rate of opioid prescribing?

A   We were really reducing the doses and accomplishing our goals.

Q   What is this chart?

A   This chart shows the monthly numbers of the patients on long term opioid therapy and it shows how we were making good strides in decreasing the amount on long-term opioids.

Q   So, did the decline in the number of patients on long-term opioid therapy shown by this chart come primarily from taking patients off of opioids?

A   Yes.

Q   Great, so were patients typically happy about primary care physicians weaning them off of opioids or suspending their prescriptions?

A   Some would feel better off of them and say so, but this was not the norm. Most were unhappy.

Q   And how did they react when they were weaned?

A   Some tried to negotiate, we would educate them on why and explain the risks and offer other therapies. Often the conversations escalated and the patient would argue. It could, and sometimes did get a little scary for the providers.

Q   Why did they react this way?

A   I think it varied on the reason for the reduction. Some of the big reactions came from those who did not have any drug in the urine. They were unhappy that they would no longer going to receive the medication. They became angry.

And then there were some that were addicted and so they got very nervous when you said you were going to reduce the dose because they were addicted. We did offer assistance and Dr. Psychologist worked closely with us and other mental health providers to try to ease their concern and everything. And we did offer them other therapy. It really depended on the reason we were reducing the dose and how they reacted.

Q   Did they complain?

A   Yes.

Q   And how did they complain?

A   Most would leave the primary care provider's office and go to the patient advocate office to complain. Then, the patient advocate would go to the primary care provider's office to try to negotiate on behalf of the patient. The other places the patient would go to complain were the director's office, the chief of staff's office, and politicians' offices.

Q   Did all of these complaints affect the FBTRHCS patient satisfaction scores?

A   Yes.

Q   And how did they do that?

A   Our scores were very low on patient satisfaction.

Q   What was the link, how was that translated to those scores?

A   The patients would get a survey in the mail and they would write how happy or unhappy they were with their primary care provider, specialty care provider, and other services. We received very low ratings for primary care providers.

Q   And how did you know that was connected to opioids?

A   The patients complained about being tapered off of opioids and this was found in the patient advocate tracking system as the reason patients were upset. And we monitor that tracking system. I had two administrative officers and they saw every report and most of the complaints did have to do with opioids.

Q   Did patients ever get violent?

A   Yes.

Q   And how did they do that?

A   I got called by a nurse one time asking for the police because they had an angry patient about his opioids and the police would respond right away. Anyone could call the police, but I happened to take the call one time from a nurse.

Q   Were you aware of any doctors that were harmed for not filling opioid prescriptions.

A   Yes, an orthopedist in our state had a woman in his office that wanted opioids and he did not give her the opioids. The husband ended up confronting the orthopedist in the parking lot and shot him. The doctor died.

Q   How did FBTRHCS top leadership react to these patient complaints?

A   They believed the patients' complaints.

Q   Did they tell you that they were unhappy about all of these complaints?

A   Yes. They would ask me to speak to certain primary care providers who were receiving more complaints than others. These providers were usually the strong opioid safety initiative providers.

Q   What do you mean when you say that someone is a strong opioid safety initiative provider?

A   They are very good at taking this initiative seriously. They have the conversations with the patients on why they need to be decreased for the different things I mentioned already. They document well in the chart and offer alternative medicines for treatment as appropriate. And they document and interpret urine drug screens well. They are kind and professional, but they hold to their decision in the name of patient safety.

Q Did Dr. Chief of Staff in particular say anything about these complaints?
A He very much believed the patients' stories and they can be very convincing and very heartfelt on their part, I'm sure, in many circumstances. So, he would often believe them and not check their medical record very well.
Q Did Mr. Director say anything to you about these complaints?
A Yes. He wanted us to believe the patients and said that he'll always believe the patients regularly. I would say about weekly. But we, as physicians, have to go on what is in the patients' medical records. And we base our decisions on doctor/patient relationships along with facts.
Q Did Mr. Director talk to you about patient satisfaction scores?
A Yes. Regularly. We reviewed a special report regularly that had quality and satisfaction measures. We performed extremely high on quality measures including low mortality rates, but that did not seem to matter to Mr. Director. He focused on patient satisfaction scores.
Q Did Dr. Chief of Staff talk about patient satisfaction?
A Yes.
Q Did Dr. Chief of Staff start to intervene in prescriptions of opioids by front-line primary care physicians?
A Yes.
Q When did he start doing that?
A Prior to my arrival. I heard that directly from primary care providers that prior to my arrival, he used to visit them quite often. And that's when he was deputy chief of staff and acting as the associate chief of staff for primary care. So, he intervened even prior to my arrival.
Q And what did he do when he intervened?
A He would go to the primary care providers and ask them to rethink their treatment plans. Once I was appointed to my position, the primary care providers or others would call me and let me know what was happening, and I would intervene on behalf of the primary care providers. He would say, "Hey, can you give them back their opioid?" or say, "Can you slow the

taper or rethink your treatment plan and do something different?" He made suggestions that made the primary care providers uncomfortable.

Q   How did you become aware of him doing that?

A   I had different calls from different providers fairly regularly.

Q   And was that inappropriate?

A   Yes.

Q   Why is that?

A   Dr. Chief of Staff, although he's a physician, he's not practicing and I don't believe he has a DEA license or experience in opioid use other than what he has learned along the way through the education at this facility. I just lost my train of thought. Will you please repeat the question?

Q   Yes, I was asking you why it was inappropriate for him to intervene?

A   Oh, yes, he doesn't know the patient's medical history. He's responding to a patient complaint without reviewing the patient's medical record.

Q   What is this exhibit?

A   This is an email message from a mental health provider to me to make me aware as the opioid safety initiative champion that Dr. Chief of Staff is intervening regarding the opioids for the patient.

Q   And are you familiar with the patient being discussed in the e-mail?

A   Yes.

Q   Are you familiar with the patient's treatment?

A   I know that he was weaned off of opioids because of his addiction problem and the primary care team was getting him help in other areas.

Q   Without talking about the patient's name, how were you familiar with this patient and his treatment?

A   I worked with the mental health provider for social work and with different people involved in his treatment.

Q   And was this patient's opioid prescription being tapered or suspended?

A   Yes.

Q   And do you recall why?

A   He was addicted.

Q   So, I'd like to draw your attention to the bottom of this e-mail chain.

Chief of Staff talks about the patient's intention of driving his car into the wall. Do you recall that event?

A   I do, yes.

Q   What do you recall of that event?

A   I remember he was angry. The patient had been tapered and a lot of people worked with him. Obviously, the mental health provider let me know about him. He had a social worker involved. Many alternative treatments were offered. It's how we do things. We offered to help him with his addiction, but he intentionally drove his car into a wall of a building. The patient endangered his life and the lives of others.

Q   And what does it mean that this email's subject title is Ms. Politician inquiry?

A   That is what we call a political inquiry.

Q   Why is Mr. Director cc'd on the email from the Dr. Chief of Staff about the individual patient's treatment?

A   Dr. Chief of Staff and I both know Mr. Director is very involved with Ms. Politician. To me, it's intimidating to have the director on the e-mail. He is not clinical, but it's like they are letting us know we need to make this patient happy. It tends to be very intimidating.

Q   Please review the next email in the chain from a political staffer.

A   Oh, okay.

Q   So, are those things that she's passing on to the patient typical of the kind of statements that patients make to doctors when they try to get their opioid prescriptions back?

A   It can be, yes.

Q   And, as a physician, how much weight do you give to patient statements like that?

A   As physicians, we check the medical record. There is more involved than simply listening to the patient. I mean, the

patient deserves to be heard, but we definitely check the medical record to see what else is involved such as what kind of
mental health history they have, medication list, other suicide
attempts or drug overdoses, whatever it might be. We review
the medical history and look at the facts.

Q Is the typical standard of care to offer a patient all of those different modalities of non-opioid pain relief?

A Yes, that is very typical.

Q And when a patient doesn't follow-up with those pain relief
options, as this here states that this patient did not, but still asks
for opioids, what does that tell you about a patient?

A It tells me that the main agenda is to get the opioids back.
The patients looking for pain relief will take us up on these
alternatives.

Q Please take a look at this email. Can you acknowledge that
this patient's treatment was appropriate for Dr. Chief of Staff
to offer this patient an opioid prescription after he had been
tapered off?

A No, it was not appropriate.

Q Was it unsafe?

A Yes, it was unsafe.

Q And was it far enough outside the standard of care that you
would consider it potentially illegal?

A Yes. Yes. As a physician, you could get in litigation trouble for
prescribing opioids for giving addicted patients opioids, especially when the patient drove his car into a wall. It's a red line
that should not be crossed. A physician could get into legal
trouble.

Q And did you confront Dr. Chief of Staff to tell him that is was
unsafe or illegal?

A Yes, I did.

Q Did you tell him he should stop intervening like this?

A Yes, I did.

Q About how many times do you estimate you talked to Mr.
Director and Dr. Chief of Staff about your concerns regarding
opioid safety?

A   Oh, let's see. For awhile, I would include an opioid safety initiative or pain management section in my weekly morning report
for primary care. I was eventually asked to stop making them
aware. Then, our service line updated them monthly which was
a requirement.

Q   Were there other issues you talked to them about being illegal
or dangerous?

A   I think I've given a lot of examples.

Exhibit J
Primary Care Recommendations

Patient being informed of a Taper of Narcotics

- Facility leadership should support the clinical decision to
taper the patient
  - Patient Safety vs. Patient Comfort…what's more
  important?
  - Support PC Leadership decision not to approve
  change of provider requests
    - Avoids Doctor Shopping
    - Prevents a new physician from being blind-sided

✓ Patient Safety
    - Provider that starts a taper needs to monitor the
    patient
✓ Patient Safety
- Primary Care Providers
  - Need to offer Alternative Treatment Options
    - Pain Management, Mental Health, Acupuncture,
    & Etc.
  - Work closely with Clinical Pharmacy

Q   Doctor, I would like you to look back to Exhibit J that we talked
about a little while ago, just above this one. It starts on page 61.

Please flip to the final page of the exhibit and that's page 87. Who is the presentation made to?

A   This is made to the executive leadership team which included the director and the chief of staff and others.

Q   And what did you discuss in conjunction with this final page of the exhibit?

A   Every month we encouraged supporting the primary care providers during tapers. We asked them to trust the primary care relationship with the patient in the clinical decision being made and to not approve change of provider requests. It was very important to understand why changing providers was unsafe for patients. We were looking for their support.

Q   What is the problem with changing providers in the middle of a taper?

A   The taper is set up better and it's monitored more closely by the original providers. If you switch providers, the new provider may not even be aware there is a taper in progress.

Q   Did opioid patients try to doctor shop?

A   Yes, they did.

I ended up going through three log books filled with patient examples and how Mr. Director, Dr. Chief of Staff, Dr. Deputy Chief of Staff and Ms. Politician interfered with patient care in relation to opioids. I gave dates, times, names of patients, and more facts than anyone wanted to see or address prior to my day in court. I reviewed dates and times when I met with senior leaders to inform them of concerns which included individual meetings, committee meetings, medical staff meetings, morning report dates and more.

The next line of questioning involved the gut-retching television news story featuring untruthful patients and Dr. Chief of Staff where my name was slandered. My photograph flashed throughout the story which seemed unending. Sickened, I forced myself to watch the story. I relived the experience as I testified.

Q   All right, Dr. Sky, are you aware of the spring 2017 news story in which you were featured?

A   Yes.

Q   And we stipulated to this particular news story, so I won't point it out, but that news story is located in Exhibit N. I entered it into the record and stipulated it already. Sir? If it's there, it's on Exhibit N. Just let me know if that the same story. And just to be clear, counsel, do you have problems stipulating that being the record also—

Q   Dr. Sky, were you asked to participate in that story?

A   Yes.

Q   Did you?

A   No.

Q   Why did you decline?

A   My husband asked me not to participate. He was concerned that the angry patients would have a face to go with my name. He was concerned about my safety, basically.

Q   Did you release your picture to the news station?

A   No.

Q   Did you tell the facility they could?

A   No.

Q   And are you familiar with the patient care of the three patients featured in the story?

A   Yes, I am.

Q   How were you familiar with these cases?

A   I was involved as part of their patient care. I reviewed their cases. And do you want me to tell you more?

Q   Yes, please.

A   I gave a detailed report of each patient explaining the reality of their situations related to opioid use.

Q   Would it have been potentially illegal or unsafe to provide these patients with the opioids they were seeking?

A   Yes.

Q   And would you have been allowed to discuss that on the air?

A   No.

Q   And did you tell Dr. Chief of Staff of the conditions?

A   Yes.

Q   Could he have looked this information up on their charts before or after the interview he did with the news station?

A   Yes.

Q   So how did you feel when you saw the story?

A   I was horrified, shocked, filled with disbelief; I felt humiliated, scared that my picture was just flashing all over the place. And I knew what the behavior could be from some of the patients, so a lot of different emotions flooded over me all at once.

Q.   Did this change the way you went out in public?

A.   Yes.

Q.   How did it affect your reputation?

A.   It really damaged my reputation. I mean, they said on there that I cut patients off at the knees when in reality, opioid changes were implemented to protect them. So, the story portrayed me as a bad, unsafe doctor and for 15 years I worked to make opioid use safer. And it just, it just, it really destroyed my reputation.

Q.   And is it still available on Google, the story?

A.   Yes.

Q.   And has anybody ever asked you about it after this?

A.   Yes.

Q.   Who is that?

A.   I actually interviewed for, actually working right now out in big sky country—and when I interviewed there, they asked me why I was looking for a job and fortunately, I shared the news story with them. They knew about the story already I learned by googling my name prior to the interview. They expressed understanding the dysfunction of the large health-care system and expressed admiring my honesty about the situation.

Q   Dr. Sky, what is this exhibit?

A   This is an automatic suspension of healthcare privileges.

Q   And how are you familiar with it?

A   Dr. Chief of Staff issued this letter in the spring of 2017.

Q   How long after the television story was that?

A   Just a couple of days.

Q   And were you surprised when you were issued the suspension?

A   More than surprised. Shocked. I couldn't believe this was happening.

Q   So, what is the suspension and how does it work when you're suspended?

A   They were suspending my health care privileges which meant I could not do my job as the associate chief of staff. Without privileges, I couldn't help with opioid safety initiatives as a prescribing champion.

Q   What exactly are privileges?

A   Privileges are part of the credentialing and privileging process granting physicians the ability to practice medicine as part of the medical staff of a hospital. Privileges are granted based upon training, experience, and such. It is something that physicians hold dear to us, to have healthcare privileges at a facility.

Q   So, were you allowed to continue supervising primary care physicians without your privileges?

A   No.

Q   So what, what exactly did the suspension document say you were being suspended for?

A   It says failure to implement opioid safety initiatives with patients in a safe and ethical manner.

Q   Were you told you'd be reported to the state licensing board?

A   Yes.

Q   And did you take that as a threat against your license?

A   Yes.

Q   And was it your medical license?

A   Yes, medical license. It's that and the National Practitioner Database too which also affects your privileging and getting a job.

Q   What could happen if you have something happen to your license?

A   You cannot practice medicine without a license.

Q   And do you think that this threat was meant to, do you think that this was meant to intimidate you?

A   Yes, I do.

Q   And what is the subject of the suspension? I should say, the subject line?

A   It says automatic suspension of healthcare privileges.

Q   Could you explain what that National Practitioner Database is?

A   Yes. NPDB is a national quality of care type of site for medicine for reporting concerns about a physician's ability to practice medicine by hospitals or legal findings. During the hiring process, that database is always checked by potential employers. So, if you have something that gets reported to the NPDB, that's National Practitioner Database, that information will be found by potential employers every time you seek employment as a physician or try to get privileges at a hospital.

Q   So, how long does that stay in your record?

A   That's forever.

Q   What is this exhibit?

A   It is an email from Dr. Chief of Staff announcing that my privileges were being fully restored.

Q   We just looked at an automatic suspension of privileges and here in this email from Dr. Chief of Staff, he calls your suspension a summary suspension. Are those two things the same thing?

A   No.

Q   Your Honor, I move to enter Exhibit P to the record.

Q   What is this exhibit?

A   The medical staff bylaws and rules regarding credentialing and privileging

Q   Let's review the documents in detail. (They all review...) So, do you think the large health care facility issued an automatic suspension of privileges or did they just call it that by mistake?

A   I think they called it that by mistake.

Q   And would you please turn to section three above, page 238. And would you please read the first sentence that begins the director has the authority?

A   The director has the authority whenever immediate action must be taken in the best interest of patient care due to potential of imminent danger to the health and well-being of an individual, including a practitioner to summarily suspend all or a portion of a practitioner's delineated clinical privileges.

Q. So, as you recall from Exhibit S, the reason given for your suspension was "failure to implement opioid safety initiatives of patients in a safe and ethical manner." Was there anything you were doing at the time of your suspension that created the "potential of imminent danger to the health and well-being of an individual" that you believe would justify a summary suspension for failure to implement opioid safety initiatives?

A No.

Q What is this exhibit?

A An internal investigation by FBTRHCS quality management medical team on patients who I helped review their opioid prescription at one of our facilities. This is a summary of how I handled the opioid prescriptions they were checking. It was done safely.

And I know that tapering was a big concern and they found that I was compliant 100 percent of the time on tapering.

Q So, could you explain in more detail what Exhibit KK found?

A They found that I followed very safe opioid safety initiative prescribing practices. That I was very safe in how I did things.

Q And can you explain a little more about what these entries mean? It's hard for a non-doctor—

A Okay. Sure. Sixty-six charts were reviewed. One of the things we do is make sure there's a valid pain agreement and it's called a valid contract here. The reviewer comments that 89 percent of the time, there was a valid contract in place. She explains the steps that were taken by me to make sure we were 100 percent compliant. Next, the reviewer comments about having a valid prescription monitoring program review to make sure patients are not doctor shopping or going elsewhere for opioids in addition to getting opioids at the large health-care system. The reviewer comments on urine drug screen compliance and puts my compliance rating at that time along with my notes. Lastly, the reviewer comments on appropriate tapering which was 100 percent compliant.

Q   What does that mean, appropriate tapering?

A   That means I tapered at a rate that was acceptable. I made sure the taper was done safely and appropriately.

Q   Who asked for the review?

A   Mr. Director.

Q   What was the date?

A   Early spring 2017.

Q   Did another leader do a review during the same time?

A   Yes. Dr. Deputy Chief of Staff was required to review the same entries. He handed the review off to his nonclinical administrative officer and she did not know her way around the clinical chart. She asked my nonclinical clerk to help her. The clerk shared with me that they had difficulty with making decisions about what to put on the chart that the Ignorant Oversight Body (IOB) used during their inspection. Dr. Deputy Chief of Staff may have reviewed the charts on his own later, but the information given to the IOB was prepared by nonclinical employees.

Q   Dr Sky, besides being suspended, were you allowed to keep your role as opioid safety champion?

A   No.

Q   When the Professional Standards Board recommended you be reinstated in the spring of 2017 did you expect to be immediately reinstated?

A   Yes, I did.

Q   Why did you expect that?

A   The Professional Standard Board is made up of a group of clinicians. They're leaders of different specialty departments, very much capable of reviewing clinical material. I expected to be fully reinstated immediately.

Q   Dr. Sky, please read this exhibit.

A   When privileges are summarily suspended, a comprehensive review of the reason for summary suspension should be accomplished within 30 days of the suspension with recommendations to proceed with formal procedures for reduction of revocation of clinical privileges forwarded to the facility director for consideration and action. In those instances where the comprehensive review cannot be accomplished in 30 days, the circumstances should be documented with an expectation of when the comprehensive review will be completed. The facility director must make a decision within five business days of receipt of the recommendations.

Q. So, were you surprised when the director didn't make a decision within five days of the receipt of the recommendation?

A. Yes in a fair world and no because I know the director's ambitions.

Q What message did that send to you when Mr. Director delayed this?

A A message of fear. I feared for the loss of my privileges and not being able to get them back.

Q Do you think this was meant to scare you?

A Yes.

Q Why do you think that?

A There would be no reason not to give me my privileges back. This felt like retaliation already just to have my privileges removed. To not get them again, I felt retaliated against again and again. I was scared that I would not get my privileges back at all.

Q So, after your privileges were reinstated, did Dr. Chief of Staff propose a reprimand against you?

A Yes.

Q Dr. Sky, why did you decide to retire from the large health-care system?

A I knew I could not go back to FBTRHCS and I was unable to secure another position within the system at another facility.

Q Why couldn't you stay at the large health-care facility?

A I really had no other choice. I wouldn't be able to follow safe opioid prescribing practices and prior I was the champion. People came to me for advice. I earned the trust of the people I worked with and they valued my expertise. But, after my privileges were removed, I was questioned about putting patients in imminent danger to others. I understood that I would no longer be an effective opioid safety leader. I felt forced to either change and prescribe the way they wanted me to prescribe or leave. I knew I couldn't follow their ways because their ways were illegal.

Q   Did you take the reprimand as a message?

A   Yes.

Q   Why did you take it as a message?

A   Their expectations were very scary, very unfair. I had my clinical privileges back and they are using a reprimand to go after me again. I felt I was a victim. I guess that's the way to say it. And I was very fearful. I couldn't go back there.

Q   Before, you mentioned that you felt free to prescribe in a way you felt was safe?

A   Yes, I definitely did. I really did.

Q   And how did your suspension and other retaliatory actions we've been discussing change that?

A   I would say they just created fear in that they would just keep trying to do something, come after me with another reprimand, counseling, suspension, no matter what I did. And even if my actions proved to be appropriate, I felt I would be retaliated against or something else was right around the corner. I just couldn't be effective as a provider and I couldn't be effective as a leader for my staff. I definitely could not be the opioid safety champion, and there was nobody else to take on that role. So, we really didn't have any protection in doing the right thing.

Q   Did other physicians leave the large health-care system during this period?

A   Yes, they did.

Q   Who?

A   Dr. PCP6 retired early from the large health-care system and went to work in the community because of opioid concerns he had. And then I know Dr. PCP7 left the large health-care system because of pressure put on her by leadership and I was no longer there to stand in the gap to support her. And then there is PCP3, NP who ended up taking a position in specialty medicine because she was one that Dr. Chief of Staff would approach. She was concerned that when I was removed, she did not have that protection again and she was concerned about opioid prescribing as well. Dr. PCP5 left the large health-care facility because she could not physically see all the patients who she needed to see face-to-face to make opioid changes.

Q   Dr. Sky, did each of these individuals confide in you and explain to you specifically why they chose to leave the large health-care system?

A   Yes, they did.

Q   Did you feel that you could make safe prescribing decisions before your suspension?

A   Yes. Yes, I felt very valued for my knowledge base and my recommendations.

Q   And did you feel that you would be able to securely make those same prescribing decisions after your suspension and later action and their retaliation?

A   No.

Q   And could you have done your job with that fear that you couldn't make the same prescribing decisions?

A   No, I would not have been an effective leader at all.

Q   Could you have done your job in any way?

A   No. Because opioids would always come up and then I would be forced to possibly do very unsafe things and that's what made me so concerned. I just did not want to be coerced into writing an unsafe prescription or not being able to interpret urine drug screens correctly and apply the right actions, safe actions, and legal actions.

Q   So, Dr. Sky, how did all these actions make you feel?

A   Oh, definitely humiliated, depressed. I didn't go out in pub-lic, and I'm a very outgoing, smiley person down the hallway, always greeting everybody, saying hello, and I really just kind of hid out. I had a hard time functioning. My family was very con-cerned. I was concerned. I was very anxious. My picture was out there, and I seemed more easily identifiable. I was concerned about that too.

Somehow, I survived. I testified to the best of my ability with the truth as I knew the truth. I silently praised the LORD.

One of my first witnesses was a primary care provider with twenty-seven years of medical experience. She started out as a military doctor, went into private practice, and also worked at the large health-care system for thirteen years. This physician worked as an emergency room physician, geriatrician, primary care provider, and hospitalist. My attorney asked questions which promoted her twenty-seven years of experience as a primary care provider and physician duties at FBTRHCS. Max established the fact that I was her direct supervisor and the chief of staff was her second line supervisor. He questioned the witness's frequency of dealing with opioid patients to which she replied, "daily." Upon arriving at the facility, she inherited a patient panel with thirty to forty percent of her patients taking opioids for chronic pain. She testified that she tried to take her patients off of opioids for chronic pain. She hadn't practiced this way throughout her twenty-seven-year career and did not want to start now. It was unsafe. This practice was not considered to be the best care for chronic pain.

Bingo. "You go, girl!" I thought.

My attorney continued questioning the witness asking about messages I sent to the providers regarding reducing the number of patients on long-term opioid therapy. She replied that I was well versed in the use of opioids for chronic pain management and I encouraged tapering or discontinuing when appropriate and able to do so. He asked if I was supportive. The witness replied that I was very supportive and I defended the providers who were trying to decrease opioids in patients and in the community against upper management who was partial to continuing high dose opioids. Max asked what kind of direction I gave to her regarding opioid treatment. She gave an example about a chart I reviewed and pointed out the taper was too quick and I gave her some helpful advice about slowing the taper and she agreed. He then asked about suspending prescriptions. The witness stated reasons would include having a negative urine drug screens and no withdrawal symptoms. This meant in such cases, the patients most likely would be misusing or diverting the medication. It is appropriate to stop prescribing. Max asked about the chief of staff's interventions with her regarding opioids and patients' treatment recommendations. She illustrated two encounters where the chief of staff strongly encouraged her to consider not tapering or increasing the number of opioids for the two patients who she considered very suspicious for drug seeking behavior. She recalled speaking to me about one encounter. She stated she followed her clinical judgment and did not follow the chief's recommendation. She felt threatened by the chief of staff during the second encounter feeling scared to stand up for her position on the topic. She recalled that she followed her clinical judgment, but she was threatened with termination if she did not decrease the number of patient complaints about her. She did not think it was appropriate for the chief of staff to order her to change opioid prescriptions elaborating that every time she writes a prescription or any other practice of medicine, she is legally responsible and her license is at stake. She stated, "It's highly inappropriate (for the chief of staff to intervene)." She continued to answer Max's questions stating she spoke with me often while I was still there about Dr. Chief of Staff's actions and that I continued to defend her decisions regarding decreasing opioids when they were appropriate. She continued and stated I would defend her against him trying to intervene.

After I left, the questions established the role of Dr. Deputy Chief of Staff in taking over my position. His message clearly differed from mine. He worried about patient complaints and not patient and community safety. This was his bottom line. She testified that Dr. Deputy Chief of Staff wrote prescriptions for opioids without seeing the patients first following patient complaints. She recalled specific examples. She discussed threats of disciplinary action and termination of employment.

The Associate Chief of Staff for Acute Medicine testified next. I admired her. Her office was next to mine and we frequently inter-acted. She maintained a professional demeanor at all times and was highly regarded by most of our staff. She considered retirement when this fiasco started; but she stayed on to help defend the medical staff. This physician worked as a medical professional for 42 years. She trained in the field of emergency medicine at a large teaching facil-ity, became head of the department for six years, appointed Deputy

Chief of Staff of the hospital for two years and then accepted the Chief of Staff position and served for over ten years.

The physician's role at FBTRHCS was outlined by my attorney. She named Dr. Chief of Staff as her immediate supervisor and Mr. Director as her second line supervisor. She described how she initially assisted in opioid safety as part of a group because it was well known they were not managing opioid patients well. As the group evolved, she stepped away.

When asked about her impression about my work on opioids, she said my work was "heroic." She stated I "was a one-person show" and I "took on an incredible amount of responsibility with unimaginable enthusiasm and competence" and that she "didn't see (me) get very much support." When asked about her role on the PSB and if she thought my privileges should have been suspended, she replied, "Absolutely not." She stated that I deserved an award for what I did and thought I single handedly took on the opioid challenge with very little support.

The questioning continued with questions centered around the summary suspension of privileges and why the witness thought this was not warranted. She replied that in her 40 years of practicing medicine, half of which included roles and ability to influence decisions, she thought the recommendation of a suspension to be "the most egregious thing" she had ever seen in her career and she told the chief of staff this very thing later during another meeting. A summary suspension of privileges would only be used if clear and imminent danger to patient care existed. She stated there was absolutely none of that in my case. She said at the PSB meeting, the chief of staff had "zero support for the summary suspension." She stated everyone in the room appeared shocked.

My colleague was asked how comfortable was she in regard to the large health care system's facility administrative leaders conducting the investigation themselves into Dr. Sky. She replied they were biased and self-serving. Max asked about the deputy chief of staff and his investigation outcome. My colleague replied the deputy stated there was no wrong-doing. She continued to elaborate on her surprise as well as the other clinical leaders' surprise at how their recommendation was ignored by the director. She continued to paint the situation as being very sad, that I was the kind of physician everyone would want to have and my leaving was a loss for the patients. She stated I lost my position on the east coast because they could not wait for all of this to resolve and how something like the summary suspension affects physicians' careers.

I was touched by Dr. ACOS for Acute Medicine's testimony. I silently praised God.

Dr. Chief of Staff was to testify next. He was sworn in (a lot of good that did in the end). He ended up being very unprepared so he was dismissed until his attorney could help him with the required documents.

We proceeded with the review of a video previously recorded by one of other physician friendly witnesses. We became good friends working together and we grew closer through all of this mess. He inspired me to write after sharing his book with me and he gave me the title of my first book, *Oh, the Things They Like to Hide*. He practices in greener pastures now also. We both praise God for the blessings in our new lives. During his interview, he was asked about my connection with him. He stated my title and task of supervision over the outpatient primary care clinics. He outlined his ten years of experience at the large health care system and the series of chiefs of staff and primary care chiefs who rarely if ever visited the clinics until I arrived. He sang my praises and I smiled watching the video as if he could see me.

Then came the opioid crisis, he described, and how we started to address narcotics in 2013. Prior to this time, monitoring the use of opioids was nonexistent. He described the changes made in the interest of opioid safety. Patients were irritated by the prescribing changes. Guidelines came requiring tapering opioids and weaning patients off of opioids altogether. He described exceptions for hospice patients and others with terminal illness or terminal cancer. He described the resistance by patients on opioids for chronic pain and their many complaints as well as other patients who expressed understanding. The violent patients who screamed, shouted, and tried to intimidate bothered him greatly. The police department became involved with some of the violent patients and he described attempts by some to attack him. He caught several patients diverting their medication.

My attorney asked about Dr. Chief of Staff's involvement during weaning situations and the witness recalled two specific incidents. The first incident occurred when he was two thousand miles away on vacation involving a very well-known difficult patient, interference by Ms. Politician, the director, the chief of staff and my helpful involvement. The chief of staff called him four or five times while he was on vacation to discuss the patient. He said he did not want the chief of staff to change his treatment plan because he indeed had a meticulously followed plan for the patient. He recalled feeling pressured by the chief of staff to go backward on the plan which would increase the dose and not decrease the dose as planned. The other incident involved an extremely difficult, extremely volatile, manipulative patient on a long-term weaning plan. The chief of staff became more and more involved in this patient's care. The patient called upon Ms. Politician's influence also. It became clear to the witness that he had to go backward on his treatment plan and increase the doses of the opioid medication to placate the patient. He documented the discussion in the medical record and how he felt this was dangerous. He documented he could not comply because the recommendation was inappropriate. He asked Dr. Chief of Staff to take over the care of the patient. Dr. Chief of Staff was not happy.

The witness outlined his ten-year career at the large health care system at a contract clinic site. He worked as a contract physician and we hired him as an employee. We interviewed him for a leadership role at the new clinic we were building in the area and processed him for hire. He completed the proper paperwork, presented for his physical, and he was on the road to becoming a company employee. He communicated regularly with the chief of staff and they were both excited about the situation at that time. They even shared thoughts about the importance of opioid safety and the launch of new programs. Then came the unexpected email from the human resource department. The company rescinded his employment offer. Dumfounded, he tried to make appointments with the chief of staff and the director. He did reach the chief of staff by telephone and received some lame explanation that there were "concerns" that had come up and he would not be a good fit at the new health care center. The witness asked the chief to be very direct with him and was told by the chief that he could not tell him anything. The chief said he would speak to the director and get back to him. He never did.

The witness wrote to the director and did not receive a reply even after sending numerous follow up emails inquiring if the director received his letter. The director ignored the letter and the emails.

My colleague stated he believed the revocation of his employment was due to opioids. He replied this was a contentious issue and he was well versed in the politics of the organization and involvement with Ms. Politician.

Dr. Chief of Staff returned and the judge reminded him that he was previously duly sworn. My other attorney, William, took over questioning the chief of staff. Following answers describing his job title, position, and what he was responsible for at the facility, and who was in charge of opioid safety initiatives at the facility, William asked what a DEA license is for. Oh my! Now I knew William's value, big time! Dr. Chief of Staff replied that he did not have a DEA license in the end. He could not prescribe opioids or other controlled substances. Although appointed chief of staff, he did not have the credentials to prescribe scheduled drugs. The chief of staff ordered others to prescribe opioids he didn't have a license to prescribe.

Many questions to the chief of staff asked him to describe the state law, facility policy, and facility practices centered around opioid safety initiative practices and face-to-face visit expectations. Reading the chief's testimony nauseates me. He spoke like a smooth-tongued snake in the grass. Lies poured out of his mouth. Political mumbo jumbo, made up expectations to cover up reality, concocted speculations about my opioid practices, and other lies gushed from the chief of staff's oral cavity. His testimony disgusted me. I pitied him. A professed man of God lied like the devil himself.

William launched his snare. He asked why the chief of staff did not do a summary suspension earlier when he first learned of the Ignorant Oversight Body's report stating I was not practicing safe opioid management. A savvy reply came forth and then his ridiculous suggestion that I should have lined up all the patients at the clinic and had a quick face-to-face visit with them. The meeting the chief of staff and I had with the clinic primary care provider from that clinic came to mind. She met with us to say she had seventy-five more patients needing face-to-face visits and there was not enough time to meet with all of her patients in a month let alone an afternoon or a day. This was just one provider at one clinic under discussion. I provided oversight for about thirty-five different providers who prescribed opioids at six different locations in the state. His expectation was ludicrous. My attorney asked the chief of staff again, "So you said you didn't summarily suspend her privileges at that point in time. Did you have any concern at that point in time for the health, welfare, and safety of the patients, based on what Dr. Sky had done when you first learned about the issue (from the IOB report)?" His question painted a clear picture. Retaliation was the motive behind my suspension two days later in response to the news story that embarrassed the director. This motive becomes even more evident following the director's testimony the following day.

My attorney sought impeachment of Dr. Chief of Staff' testimony. He questioned the chief's understanding of giving complete and accurate testimony to which he responded, "Yes." William tried to impeach Dr. Chief of Staff in regard to conflicting testimony where the chief said he gave me written counseling and later testified that he only gave me verbal counseling. Dr. Chief of Staff squirmed out of that one stating he thought he gave me written counseling previously and since concluded that it must have been verbal with an air of believable crap. He escaped William's trap. William would later ensnare the director.

William established through Dr. Chief of Staff's testimony that he was not an opioid expert. His role was administrative in nature and not clinical. After eliciting responses as to why the chief of staff went against the unanimous clinical recommendation of the PSB members due to imminent danger to patients to summarily suspend my privileges, William continued. He summarized the chief's previous testimony and William questioned the chief about having previously talked about not having a DEA license and how he was not an opioid expert, why would he go against the recommendations by clinicians on the PSB? The chief of staff stated the PSB did not make a recommendation. They chose not to support his recommendations. He dismissed the importance of a DEA license and stated he knows the fundamentals of patient care. He carried on spewing a distorted view of his reasoning behind the suspension. I admit, he can sure sling excrement with an unbelievable fragrance of rose blossoms.

Opposing counsel asked Dr. Chief of Staff many questions. I failed to see any significant point to her questions. I noted that she asked him about being disciplined and he replied that he had by the director. He stated he received a letter for failure to provide sufficient direction since he could not provide documentation or instruction of communicating with me about my medical practice and opioid prescription. That honest statement concluded his overall perjured testimony. It was now 6:55 p.m. We were all exhausted.

The following day, Mr. Director sat in the hot seat. As he sat waiting for the official start to the day's hearing, he conversed in nonsensical ingenuine conversation with his attorney, completely avoiding eye contact with me. I sat quietly, despising the puffed-up man yet trying deeply to forgive him for his insincere actions. I remained calm, knowing my testimony was behind me and his was just beginning. I could not wait to see what my attorneys planned for their most important witness. Mr. Director was duly sworn by the judge. Impeachment would soon materialize.

Mr. Director answered questions about the opioid safety initiative and the opioid crisis in America, opioid flags, the need for collaboration between a doctor and a patient, and he responded to the question of always believing the patient in the negative. William directed the witness to documentation of a previous inquiry. He reminded Mr. Director that he was under oath at that time also and the importance of being truthful. He testified that he was angry about his fellow patients being labeled as drug seekers when they are in pain and that I created a drug seeking culture in primary care. He stated at that time, "we defer to the side of the (patient)." He admitted this was his testimony.

William redirected his questioning to the news story on television, asking about his reaction to the story. Mr. Director replied basically this was no big deal and we were always in the media up to twelve times a month. He stated he does not overreact. He moves on. He was asked to elaborate and elaborate he did about a multitude of incoming media inquiries for a variety of reasons and a response is coordinated through a public affairs officer or with the regional office. Carefully constructed (politically correct self-serving, my words) responses are provided to the inquiries. My attorney asked the director what his response was to the news story on television in relation to me and if he took action. He said, "no action."

William asked Mr. Director to turn to an exhibit as he read from Mr. Director's previous testimony to another investigator, "…something has to happen to Dr. Sky, positive or negative or indifferent, but there needs to be a look at it. When the political pressure came…kind of yesterday…there needs to be a PSB today, and I want to see the memos…I'm going to see the minutes…But again, the whole PSB in unison, the PSB deferred on any actions against Dr. Sky….there could be a suspension which sends a statement that we adhere to policy." Then, the clincher, "I have the newspaper articles, you know, staple it to the suspension guidance." William recapped stating, "So, you were saying that you wanted to staple a copy of the newspaper to the suspension as proof of why there should be a suspension?"

Mr. Director went on to say that the three patients in the article had concerns, the three untruthful patients that nobody checked facts prior to airing the story on television and writing a newspaper article about false testimonies. The director rambled on about the death of a patient who had been proven to have died from a massive heart attack weeks after he was tapered off of opioids. The director still held onto the lie that the patient died from the opioid taper despite the fact the case had been sent for review twice and my actions were justified twice clinically.

The Ignorant Oversight Body report kept coming up too which was completely inaccurate with conclusions based upon senior leadership testimony and omission of clinical testimony which would have damaged the facility's reputation. Senior leaders and investigating bodies participated in a grand cover-up scheme to protect the facility and large health care system in general. The truth would cut their conclusions to the quick. The giant would fall. David slayed the giant in reality and so did my attorneys and I.

My former administrative officer testified next from his new position at another facility within the large health care system. He left the facility due to the upheaval centered around opioid safety. I sang his praises when his new bosses asked me for a reference. I thanked God for the friendly face after enduring Mr. Director's pompous responses.

My attorney solicited his background and job description while serving at Facility by the River Health Care System. He spoke about interacting with the executive leaders at FBTRHCS on a weekly basis. His duties included handling patient complaints from multiple levels fielding shots from patient advocates, our primary care office, the chief of staff's office, the director's office, and politicians' offices. He also assisted in opioid safety initiative efforts, presenting data monthly to the executive leadership team. These overwhelming duties monopolized his time and took away from the day to day operations of the primary care service line. Then, the big answer to one of my attorney's questions. The witness stated, "…in my humble opinion, the perception was more important than the actual safety of the patient …"

When Mr. Director, Dr. Chief of Staff, and Dr. Deputy Chief of Staff became involved in pushing unsafe agendas in order to please the patient in lieu of patient safety, the witness stated he brought situations to the ethics committee. He gave examples describing discussions with providers who stated Dr. Chief of Staff would approach them and ask them to give the patients their opioids and the patients were not assigned to that particular provider. The patients' primary care providers were tapering or suspending the opioids for valid reasons, the patients complained, and Dr. Chief of Staff asked a different provider to fill the opioid. Mr. Administrative Officer stated, "So, it just kind of demonstrated that they were just trying to keep the patient happy and give them the opioids that they were already given, even though the assigned provider was making the decision to start the taper and start to remove them off of their opioids." He named the concerned providers for the record and described the scenarios. His testimony shined a brilliant light on the reality of the pathetic actions by leaders who valued patient satisfaction over patient safety.

My attorney readied another sting for the next witness, Dr. Deputy Chief of Staff. By the time of this hearing, this guy got his story straight. He learned I knew the first clinical review of the patients involved in the Ignorant Oversight Body's review was done by a secretary and his nonclinical assistant and stated this fact. Originally, this fact was covered up in previous testimony. I testified to this fact in other interviews. He stated he did the second review. His only concern was the well-rehearsed failure to have a face-to-face visit with all of the opioid patients which he himself does not do! It's impossible. We need help from our nursing staff, clinical pharmacy specialists, other providers to communicate results and clinical recommendations. Plus, there was no such policy about a face-to-face requirement. This requirement originated from a nurse executive because the nursing staff complained. Dr. Chief of Staff relayed this information to me regularly prior to all the political attention and even told a concerned provider she cannot see all of the patients face-to-face. He told her to have the nursing staff assist her when she conferenced us about not having seventy-five slots one month to see everyone. The fake policy, fake requirement, fake expectations were part of well-rehearsed testimonies. I have to say; the liars were fairly consistent.

My attorney questioned the deputy chief of staff's expertise in opioid safety and knowledge. He was asked if he had any specialized training in opioids beyond what a regular primary care physician would have. Forced to give a yes or no answer, he said, "no." My attorney asked him to speak up and he repeated the question and required the answer again. This answer contradicted previous testimony and William uncovered this information. My attorney reminded him that he testified that there is no circumstance where he would suspend a patient's opioid prescription rather than taper. Max showed Dr. Deputy Chief of Staff the testimony. Impeachment loomed. The witness's testimony during this hearing contradicted a previous testimony. I sighed with relief. The cover up became more transparent.

The next unfriendly witness is not even worth mentioning. I could tell the agency worried about the fact that they released my photograph to the press without my permission. This violated policy blatantly. By this time in my case, I knew their angle centered around the facility's Facebook account where they posted the picture in the past they say. I just plain didn't care. Their explanation constituted one more lie heaped on the mile-high pile of lies.

The finale came next, closing remarks. The judge assigned the attorneys a finite time limit. Max flew through his closing remarks. He had so much to say in such a brief moment of time. I took a deep breath and prayed. He began with "… the agency is hiding a bad thing. The whistleblower risks everything to expose that bad thing." He spoke about how I "led a successful effort to reduce long-term opiate prescription rates at (FBTRHCS)" which created "a signif-icant backlash especially among patients who are addicted or who were diverting." He pointed out the chief of staff's testimony and how he "intervened on behalf of patients who complained loudly 'at the director's urging.' The chief of staff did this even though he was not treating those patients, even though he not have a DEA license, even reversing tapers or suspensions putting patients' lives in dan-ger, and even though it risks breaking very serious state and federal laws, even criminal laws governing the proper management of opioid drugs."

Max pointed out my repeated confrontations with the chief of staff and the director about opioid safety concerns as the in-house opioid expert at FBTRHCS. I told both of the senior leaders the interventions were illegal and dangerous. My testimony provided specific examples of multiple cases in great detail backed up by exhib-its for the record. He related how the disclosures contributed to the agency's retaliatory actions directed at me. He pointed out the weak-nesses in the agency's justification for the retaliatory actions. He illus-trated the suspension reasons provided occurred the year prior and had not continued since as testified by the chief of staff so why was I an imminent threat to patient care at the time of the suspension? The Ignorant Oversight Body report excuse didn't fly because it wasn't even brought to the PSB plus the IOB did not request a summary suspension of my privileges. The timeline of the report was off too. The IOB report came out two months prior to my suspension and I wrote the action plan response for the facility!

Max questioned Dr. Chief of Staff's credibility. Dr. Chief of Staff's statements contradicted my testimony and two other primary care physicians' testimonies backed up by exhibits for the record. The chief of staff offered contradictory reasons as to the delay in reinstatement of my privileges, waiting for one patient chart review during one testimony and legal determination in another. The television news story clearly showed intent to blame me as the chief of staff pointed a finger at me.

My attorney drilled holes backed by governing legal factors into the agency's reasons for why they suspended my privileges. They failed to prove imminent danger as their justification using vague explanations. He tied in Dr. ACOS for Medicine's testimony as a very credible witness, passionately stating, "the summary suspension of privileges was an outrageous abuse (of power)" She subjected herself to retaliation by testifying at the hearing. "By the way, (she) called Dr. (Sky) a hero for doing what she did." She testified, "that the summary suspension of privileges was one of the most egregious summary suspension (she) had ever seen…"

Mr. Director's testimony nailed his intention to suspend my privileges two days after the television news story and newspaper story when he said, "Staple the news story to the suspension." The director lied during his testimony that very same day. He said the news story had nothing to do with any action against me. Then, he stated the agency should "staple the news story to the suspension." The director based his decisions on a newspaper story. As a director, he had the responsibility to look at the medical record itself to validate patients' statements. Mr. Director said he wanted to send a statement. This is not what suspension of privileges is for. Suspension of privileges is to prevent imminent harm. The agency had no evidence to justify the suspension of my privileges.

Mr. Director's goal was clearly to "quiet patient complaints and improve patient satisfaction." Dr. Chief of Staff only intervened when patients complained. I clearly interfered stating the leaders' actions were illegal, unsafe which prevented the director from getting what he wanted, patient satisfaction. Political pressure and the IOB report were motives to retaliate. The director testified about all of the pressure and that the PSB had to meet today. The director and chief of staff wanted to do the "easier thing for themselves at the expense of the health of patients." I "stood up and said that's not okay, stop doing that, that is why they weren't happy with (me) in this case."

The agency's closing remarks proved to be very generalized and without substance. They failed to include exhibits to back their defense. They failed miserably. It was clear the agency retaliated against me as a whistleblower. I'm not fond of the term whistleblower, it sounds negative when in reality, to be a whistleblower takes courage, initiation, preparation and prayer. Truth must be the motivating factor. The absence of truth is why the agency should lose the lawsuit and the presence of truth is why we should win.

A year has passed and we continue to wait for the judge to rule on the case. He said during our departure from the hearing that he would rule in about three months. At the three-month mark, the judge requested a one month stay. Since that request, silence. I Googled the judge's name recently thinking he may have resigned, retired, or God forbid, died. He appears to be alive and well, still working in the same position. I'm not pushing for a ruling necessarily. I understand when the agency loses, and they should lose by all accounts, they can appeal. The Appeals Board for the Legal Battle Board has two out of three vacancies. The third member works on cases full time; but the cases just sit because three members must be present for the appeals ruling. This third member is retiring soon and the board will be completely unoccupied. The political state of affairs of the country fails to find this board to be of any importance as evidenced by their failure to appoint new members. Additionally, I believe a ruling in our favor would just be too much for the large health care system to handle. Can you imagine headlines such as: Dr. Sky uncovers opioid safety concerns which led to multiple patient deaths; Politician in the river state motivated to cover up opioid deaths to obtain votes; Director and Chief of Staff choose patient satisfaction over quality medical care adding to the opioid crisis in America....stay tuned, news at 10:00 p.m. These thoughts pass through my mind as we wait. In the end, I believe God will bring goodness to us and glory to himself. My puny little mind cannot even fathom God's plan in all of this drama. I witnessed a dark side to professionals claiming to have integrity, respect for others, commitment to the mission, and advocacy for patients and staff caring for those patients we serve. The commitment to lie, band together like hoodlums, cover-up truth, discard engaged employees, and then continue in their positions as if nothing ever happened completely illustrates where this world is heading. My prayer is that we as Christians, band together like the brothers and sisters we are and pray, pray, pray. Pray for our country. Pray for our leaders. Pray for our people. May we all recognize the sacrifice of our Lord Jesus Christ, His resurrection, and His rule. Ultimately, He will judge each and everyone's actions and hearts.

Afterword

In July of 2019, the Office of Inspector General (OIG) released a report titled, "Alleged Interference and Failure to Comply with Pain Management Directive and the Opioid Safety Initiative at (Facility by the River Health Care System)" The chief of staff was found to have interfered with applying opioid safety measures. The report included specific examples. Leaders and the system lacked requirements to implement goals of the national system. The OIG report contained forty-nine pages of impressive information containing an executive summary, introduction, scope and methodology, inspection results, conclusion, and recommendations. The investigation expanded a two-year period.

The chief of staff retired shortly after the OIG released the report. He was to answer to a national ethics board. The director received multiple recommendations for improving the facility's pain management program, education to providers regarding opioid safety, change of provider requests, and compliance monitoring. As far as I know, Mr. Director is still employed.

My attorney submitted the report to the administrative judge since he had not ruled on my case. The judge has since relocated to another state. We will continue wait on the LORD knowing that in His time, He will bring Glory to God and good to us.

Acronyms

AB	Administrative Board
ACOS	Associate Chief of Staff
AJ	Administrative Judge
AO	Administrative Officer
AO-IOB	Accountability Office to the Ignorant Oversight Body
CDC	Center for Disease Control
CDO	Complaint Department Office
CEB	Clinical Executive Board
COS	Chief of Staff
CPAP	Continuous Positive Airway Pressure
DCOS	Deputy Chief of Staff
ED	Emergency Department
ELT	Executive Leadership Team
ERCP	Endoscopic Retrograde Cholangiopancreatography, a radiology diagnostic study
ERO	Equal Rights Organization
ES	Employee Survey
ESV	English Standard Version Bible
FBTRHCS	Facility by the River Health Care System
FMLA	Family and Medial Leave Act
FOIA	Freedom of Information Act
FPPE	Focused Professional Practice Evaluation
GDO	Grievance Division Office
GI Bill	This bill passed in 1944 for bringing educational benefits to WWII Veterans and still exists.
GMO	General Medical Officer
HFO	Hassle Free Office
HIPAA	Health Insurance Portability and Accountability Act of 1996

HR	Human Resources
ICU	Intensive Care Unit
IOB	Ignorant Oversight Body
KJV	King James Version Bible
LBB	Legal Battle Board
MBA	Master of Business Administration
MRCP	Magnetic Resonance Cholangiopancreatography, a radiology diagnostic study
NIV	New International Version Bible
NLT	New Living Translation Bible
NPDB	National Practitioner Data Bank
NRA	National Rifle Association
OC	Outpatient Clinic
OIG	Office of Inspector General
OPPE	Ongoing Professional Practice Evaluation
OSI	Opioid Safety Initiative
PCP	Primary Care Provider
PMP	Prescription Monitoring Program
PSB	Professional Standards Board
RN	Registered Nurse
VTel	Video Telecommunications

About the Author

Dr. B. Sky joined a supportive medical team in heavenly big sky country in the fall of 2017. She relocated to the West most recently from the Midwest with her supportive husband, David, after working for the large health care system and other related agencies as a primary care physician and leader.

This is Dr. B. Sky's second book and reveals her true story as a whistleblower. Dr. Sky endured retaliatory consequences by executives for reporting unsafe opioid prescribing practices and lack of appropriate monitoring for chronic pain patients receiving opioids at the hospital. She outlines political and media scandal to increase patient satisfaction at the expense of patient safety resulting in unintentional opioid overdose and death of patients and people in the community. Initially her goal as an author was to outline the enormous obstacles and tedious process of navigating the systems put in place to protect employees by the agency and the high financial and emotional cost in response to ethical and moral reports. What transpired unknowingly is insight regarding mind-numbing political processes; ineffective agencies failing to help whistleblowers they were created to support; never-ending cover up schemes by deceitful people in positions of power; and most importantly, the fact that she is not alone.

Dr. B. Sky now realizes that she evolved from a naïve physician trying to help her primary care staff and opioid expert failing to protect patients and the community to an educated by fire advocate daring to expose the opposition. She understands clearly the retaliatory knee-jerk responses by executives and politicians in response to undesirable political and media scrutiny.

Dr. Sky developed empathy for other whistleblowers whose plights are significantly worse than her own including those who are criminally investigated, prosecuted, charged, imprisoned, or exiled. Several whistleblowers fared well winning their cases. One brave woman received a victorious award including millions of dollars, but this is not the norm. Most whistleblowers wait years for justice suffering job losses, tarnished reputations, financial bankruptcy, broken relationships, isolation, and loss of their freedom and never receive the outcome they deserve. Retaliation predominates. Justice is not served.

Dr. B. Sky's golden thread is her faith that God will ultimately bring glory to himself and good to the whistleblower. Without trusting God and instilling faith in Jesus Christ, fear would ensue. However, fear is a liar and God is in control. The author's goal now is to encourage others to find strength through Christ, to put on the armor of God daily, pray without ceasing, and to fight the good fight for the glory of God.

CPSIA information can be obtained
at www.ICGtesting.com
Printed in the USA
JSHW032241271220
10548JS00002B/10